Scenes from a Single Mom

Stories Collected by

Tiffany Huff-Strothers

The Tiffany Huff Experience

Coraopolis, PA

Table of Contents

Scene I: Fulfillment

Bag Lady

By Danielle L. King

Have you ever heard the saying, "You want to make God laugh? Tell Him your plans." Well, let's just say God is the original King of Comedy. All my life, I prided myself on planning. In high school, students are conditioned to start life planning in 10th grade. Then in college, your first-year seminar, your first assignment, everyone asks you "What's your five-year plan?"

Plans, plans, plans. They are BULLSHIT.

Plans are a cognitive façade we become confidently convinced about, but society fails to tell you that in this fickle world, plans get derailed daily.

Want to know my five-year plan? Yeah, me too. What was I thinking trying to override God's lifetime plan for me with a five-year plan of my own? My five-year plan included a banging job, graduating from a doctoral program in three years, cutting ties with a rebound, finding my husband, moving out of Pittsburgh, and purchasing a house.

Guess how much of that plan made the cut: Nada. Nothing. Zilch. Zero.

God has a funny way of getting your attention. Actually, it wasn't all that damn funny. God's plan for me included a six-year-long doctoral journey, financial hardships, two kids at the same damn time (in my Future voice), a lifetime of healing, and a "Rufus" (aka the Rebound). A Rufus is a habitually unemployed, invisible father, who is most likely missing a front or side tooth, if you were wondering.

"Alexa, play 'Bag Lady' by Erykah Badu." I think I played that song about 104 times a week throughout my life but hadn't really *listened* to it. Background music. Cleaning music. Getting over heartbreak music. A lullaby for the twins because they love Badulla Oblongata like they muva.

I heard that song on a random playlist while sitting on my bedroom floor, holding and feeding my three-month-old sons. I realized I had only heard the song my whole life, but I had never listened. God has a way of using your pain for a purpose, and I had to go through all I had gone through to be in that moment, to hear Him.

"Bag lady you goin' hurt your back

Draggin' all 'em bags like that

I guess nobody ever told you

All you must hold on to

Is you, is you, is you...

If you start breathin', you won't believe it

You'll feel so much better, so much better baby

Bag Lady, let it go, let it go, let it go, let it go..."

Do you mean to tell me the only thing I needed to hold onto was myself? In the words of my grandmother, "Well, I be damned." Holding onto what I thought was love was hindering me mentally, physically, and spiritually. Let it go like Elsa, Danny. Let. It. GO.

My pastor said, "A distorted image of love can be manipulated in a functional setting that will hinder you from the Lord's plans to prosper you." Pastor Wesley was onto something.

I questioned myself: "How did I get here? Where was I going? What was happening?" The crazy thing was, though, I was supposed to be there. We have free will to do whatever we want, right? I was getting my Free Willy on. Splish, splash! But, my distorted image of love came from me not loving myself. Period. I'm not about to hit you with a sonnet, a Haiku, a nothing. Flat out, I didn't love myself. I realized a love for myself didn't exist because if it had, I wouldn't have settled for breadcrumbs when I was the whole loaf, as Moneybagg said.

I reminisced on all the times I prayed over this situation and God provided ways out that I never took. Looking back on all the times outcomes confirmed intuition, I felt stupid that I never trusted myself. I had convinced myself otherwise in situations I placed myself in. Doing things I never thought I'd do. Going places I never thought I'd go. Saying things I never thought I'd say, all in the name of a distorted image of love.

I settled for an unbalance and was stuck in a routine of unreciprocated love. Then just like that, it was gone two days after my birthday. The sudden and unexpected death of a loved one, relationship, or drug habit forces you into a "cold turkey" space. Anyone who has ever tried to go cold turkey on something understands that the first time usually doesn't go so well (for those who got it the first time, kudos). Well, my drug was gone, and 40 days later, I was introduced to a rebound, which served as my relapse.

Toxicity was my drug of choice—born from relationships with broken men born from trauma. It was the "Two-Third Experience," where two good things overshadow the real problem. An example is good sex and nice gifts, but the person is a serial cheater. Or, the person is gifted and talented but won't work. Maybe they have good credit and are successful, but they are also narcissistic and misogynistic. You feel me? You settle, and their trauma becomes yours.

The perfect amount of toxicity can make you feel like you're floating and drowning at the same time. When you're up, you're up, and when you're down, well, you know the rest. I took my toxicity straight up, with no chaser. Lack of communication. Lack of loyalty, support, and commitment. Control. Dishonesty. Disrespect. All take, no give, and settling for the bare minimum.

A rebound is familiar, and in the same sense, unknown. It's effective, yet inoperative. Familiarity settled in the toxicity. You assume you can manage things you're used to. You think it's working out; however, if something is inoperative, it doesn't work. In this case, figuratively and literally. This rebound served as my new dose of toxicity. As I struggled to find peace from the trauma of my previous relationship, I was vulnerable. Like a parasite looking for a host, I needed to be in connection with someone who fit the profile I wanted—someone who was handsomely broken.

It was fried chicken and No Limit records under an October moon that brought us together, but it was *2 Kings* that connected us for life. What began as a "hood fairy tale" slowly descended into the pits of hell. I had convinced myself that love was involved, but love didn't exist.

Want a quick tip? The heart is a big liar, and sometimes it calls your mind for backup to play tricks on you, too. But ooh, intuition is Brickhouse bad. Curves on a coke bottle, lip gloss poppin' on a hot summer day, bad. Powder blue, Rocawear suit, white Nike bad. Intuition overrides everything and motivates you to assess the facts that override those feelings, but when you aren't in the space of loving yourself and leave it in the hands of someone who has never loved themselves, it's like watching a train wreck in slow motion.

I told my intuition to get in the trunk like K.C. and Brooklyn did Dolla Bill in *The Player's Club*. I told my lying ass heart, anxiety, and naivety to take the wheel as I got in the back seat. I'll tell you now, those three ugly broads totaled my car and left me stranded on the side of the road. I would say that when I see them, I owe 'em a box on-site, but I hope I never see them heauxs again. As I joyrode with those losers, we traveled farther and farther away from who I was, in unwarranted territory. I ain't have "it" on me, nothing. Out here, naked.

I tried to convince myself and those around me that my situation was different than what it was. It was a trigger to hear the opinions of others, knowing they were actual facts. I convinced myself of a lie, blaming it on potential and what I *thought* was love. The potential to be a great parent, but you can't. The potential to be a hardworking individual, but you won't. The potential to put the well-being of others before yourself, but you don't. Ha! Potential? Whew! Never entertain that nut. Potential is supposed to be action in theory, not a vision. Do as you say, feel me?

Days turned into months, months into years, and there we were, like a bad song on repeat. One thing I thought I could do was balance, but my homeboys Merriam & Webster define balance as "being able to move or remain in a position without losing control." Well, God needed me to move, and I had to lose control to do it. The control I lost served as a catalyst for the control I gained, or shall I say the peace I lost served as a catalyst for the peace I gained. When toxicity levels are in the red zone, you are forced into a place of reflection and revelation.

"Bag lady, you goin' hurt your back, draggin' all them bags like that..."

Those closest to me know I am a lifelong learner. I love to learn. Out of 34 years on this earth, 24 of 'em I spent inside a classroom. As if a bachelor's and master's degree weren't enough, I just had to go back for my doctorate. The opportunity was a blessing and something I prayed hard for. Unbeknownst to me, this journey I prayed so hard for would be the most challenging journey I would encounter thus far. I knew it would be a lot of work, but DAYUUUUMMMMMM (in my Martin Lawrence voice). I know I said, "Use me God," but this journey couldn't come with an assistant? Reading, writing, and rebounding became part of my daily routine. When I wasn't reading, I was writing. When I wasn't writing, I was reading. And when I wasn't doing either, I was rebounding...heavy.

The funny thing about my lifelong learning journey is that with all the education in the world, I still made decisions that weren't so smart, like entertaining a rebound I knew provided no substance to my life. Don't judge me, judge ya mama. Experience happened to be my favorite teacher since I took her class so many times. Rebounding was fun for a while—joyriding without a care in the world and ignoring all the construction zones, potholes, and one-ways I knew existed in this situation. Lack of self-love contributes to rough paths, but I learned that life is about choices and growth. We can choose to take whatever path we want, but we also must learn the acceptance of taking an "L." The experiences on those paths may cause physical, emotional, financial, and spiritual wear and tear, but how you respond is also your choice. Well, spoiler alert: my bounce back was better than a dribble.

As I balanced school, an inconsistent, dead-end relationship, and my strange addiction to collecting as many W2s as possible, I never realized how my love for myself was non-existent or how I was insane. Insanity is doing the same thing, repeatedly, and expecting different results. I was familiar with this ride, yet, I thought I could change the direction. Crazy, right? Why would I keep myself in a situation when God provided me with exit strategies? Why would I continue to entertain a situation I knew would have painful moments? I could ask myself these questions all day, but I still wouldn't have an answer to them. What I do know is that intuition predicted my outcome, but I put her ass in the trunk, remember?

My life's schedule was school, work, work, rebound. School, work, work, rebound. School, work, work, rebound. No period.

September birthday celebrations served as a segue to life formation, and I became pregnant. My body was now an incubator for a child (as in one, I thought) whom we would meet in June. I was excited but naive to think my situation would be any different. I chose to ignore the precedent that was set. November 15, 2018 was one of the scariest, yet most joyous days of my life. "Congrats Danielle, you're having twins." As I lay on the table in disbelief and the rebound "moonwalked" around the hospital room, my mind went crazy with thoughts and emotions. My first thought was similar to Ike Turner's reaction when Lorraine popped up and dropped them kids off to him and Tina, "WHAT I'M GOIN' DO WITH TWO MO KIDS?" (Although, they were my first). I cried. I thought about work, school, and my finances. "OMG, two of everything? Oh, shit! How can I afford school *and* TWO kids?" I thought about how I always wanted my own family—just me, my babies, and my man taking on life by force—but dang God...You wild for this one!

Then everything came to a stop.

As I watched the rebound smile and celebrate, it hit me like a freight train: I would be doing this by myself. How dare he celebrate the life he helped create, knowing that he planned to be absent? How dare I expect this time to be different from him? One of the most difficult things is living a nightmare and still having to show up with your head held high and your crown on straight.

During my pregnancy, I often spent time alone. I was conflicted about how I felt. I promised myself that if I was in a negative space, I would try my best not to stay there because I didn't want my babies to feel that energy. Talking to my friends and family about the twins was exciting, but I cried when I was alone. Hard. Deep down, I felt ashamed, embarrassed, and stuck. The signs were clear as day, and I chose to ignore them. My anxiety made me feel as if everyone else knew I'd be doing it on my own as well. I felt like I fell into a rabbit hole of "I-Told-You So"s accompanied by whispers and giggles. I hid from the world as depression crept in like a thief in the night. I was Bag Lady, for sure. I had a book bag, a bag of healing that needed to be handled, two diaper bags, two work bags, and a huge Hefty trash bag.

I became an expert in hiding my feelings. I appeared strong to my family. I came off as unbothered to my friends. I was happy around my coworkers, but the four walls of my home watched me crumble into nothing. It was my bedroom carpet where I left my knee prints from praying. It was my pillow that caught my tears. Being confined to your pessimistic thoughts is a terrible place to be. The opinions of others didn't even matter anymore—they no longer posed a threat. No external threat could compare to the negative thinking that consumed me. It was my mind that became my worst enemy.

As life continued to grow inside me, negative thinking did as well. See, when you try to control situations, your plans are derailed, you're in a place of being tormented by your thoughts, and you have no idea where you are going or how you are getting there, the *only* thing you can do is surrender. Cliché as it may sound, just surrender. Give it up. Truth be told, surrendering was tough for me. I was already in a place of uncertainty, and to completely give it to God seemed a bit much for me. I'm nosey—once I pray, I like to stay on the email thread to see how God is working. But this assignment required me to send God my prayer and remove myself from being "CC"ed.

His work was none of my business.

As God continued to author my story, I tried my best to mind my business, wobbling from the Duquesne University parking garage to a class on the third floor of a building on the other side of campus at 8:30 on Saturday mornings, still working two jobs Monday through Friday, and preparing myself for motherhood every day. It's funny how fast nine months fly by. On June 4, 2019, my son, formerly Twin A, made a cameo in the middle of a turkey sandwich, potato salad, salt-n-vinegar chips, and a deep phone conversation with my best friend, Kaylah, who invited him to the party.

He interrupts those same things to this day.

As I took my good old time making my way to the hospital, I notified the rebound that our Prime packages were on the way. Two healthy Kings (both totaling 12 pounds) made their grand entrance on June 5, 2019 after 13 hours of labor (11 of which I slept). Both head down, vaginal delivery, full-term, and only needing one stitch. I was a Magee Women's Hospital superhero that day.

The feeling of meeting your babies after giving birth is an intimate, spiritual, and amazing experience. I met these two amazing little humans with whom I had a relationship since their DNA hit a pregnancy test. Delivering them was bittersweet. I finally met them after waiting so long for them to be delivered earth-side, but I knew I couldn't protect them from the world's dangers the way I did for the past nine months. It was like Christmas. I was so tired, but I could not stop staring and praying over them. I completely forgot about everything outside of their existence. It was almost like I got my memory zapped like in *Men in Black*. Nothing else mattered but them.

Time in the hospital after labor is a three-day vacation. People wait on you hand and foot. You order anything you want to eat. You get to wear diapers that feel like California Kings on your butt. Just an overall amazing experience. Four stars. However, when you leave to go home, that's when real life starts, and for me, life got real, real quick. The rebound seemed like he kind of enjoyed them. Something to do when he was bored or photograph for a Facebook flex because creating a false sense of reality for people who don't really know you is a lot easier than creating a reality for those who do. Note to self: Watermark pictures.

I reflected on conversations regarding his relationship with his older children. Common themes surfaced during my reflection on those conversations and my own experiences. He never had a story to tell about his child after they turned one. Every story ended with his child lying on his chest, and that's just how our story ended, with both Kings laying on his chest before turning one. There was no story to tell after that. When they turned one, he retired, only to make an appearance on the 156th day of the year to pay for his annual membership.

Being a single mother to twins, working two jobs, and being in a doctoral program was my norm. "Tired" was my nickname. "Who was Sleep? Where was he from? I don't know him. When you see him, tell him get at me." I love being a mother and love my babies with everything in me, but truth be told, two-parent households need to be normalized. Or at least the household should come with a nanny. After giving birth, a woman's body is a new vessel, stabilizing chemical levels that existed before you were a human incubator. It takes time, and with two crying babies who wanted milk 24/7, working, writing a dissertation, and lacking sleep, things can get a little uneasy. Hell, I'm being modest; that shit was hard.

I found myself angry at the rebound many times. "Why does he get uninterrupted sleep? How come he still gets to have a social life?" It was more jealousy than anger, mainly because I was so tired, and he had no clue what that felt like. I soon learned that comparison is the greatest robber of joy. Being too focused on what you don't have and what others might have makes you miss your blessings. I may be tired, but the joy of seeing Gavin and Carter laugh every day brings me unexplainable joy. They're my highest thought and my grandest feeling. I have a peace that cannot be disturbed, regardless of how tired I may be.

A piece of advice: Check in on your people because you don't know what's going on, MIND YOUR BUSINESS because you don't know what's going on, and pray for people because you don't know what's going on.

My journey of motherhood wasn't easy, and I reached a breaking point. I felt consumed by my tasks and thoughts. I cried, but only when my babies were asleep. I needed a shift mentally, spiritually, and emotionally. I begged God to release me from my envy, anger, and rage. I pleaded for peace and clarity, and I prayed for strength. I said, "God give me strength." Let me tell you, those four words are the most powerful words I've ever spoken. I consistently prayed for strength, clarity, and peace with intention. I didn't receive them overnight, but I felt the shift when I did. I began to purge every piece of negativity that had held onto my existence—fear, anxiety, doubt, uncertainty, insecurity—everything I needed to be liberated from so I could fully embrace motherhood and not carry any trauma over the threshold to my new journey.

Unfortunately, but fortunately, COVID-19 provided the opportunity for me to cocoon. Mothering, studying, praying, and meditating became my new norm. It's still a work in progress, but the keywords are "in progress." Some days are better than others. Ironically, on my bad days, my dad would pop up outta nowhere with life lessons.

Now, I realize that was God.

In 2021, Gavin was diagnosed with Epilepsy. As a parent, you would give your life to protect your children with no question, but to watch your child be sick and know there is nothing you can do about it is one of the worst feelings in the world. Due to his diagnosis, I had to take a sabbatical from work to care for him, and during my sabbatical, I received no income. In addition to being a lifelong learner, I have always worked at least two jobs. This was my sense of security. So, being unemployed and providing for my family was scary.

I asked God many times to make sense of my situation. I felt like He had abandoned me because I couldn't hear Him.

Then, my car stopped working.

OK, God. Are these my battles? Am I getting someone else's hate mail? Make it make sense, Jesus!

Really? My car AND my income. You just want me to stay home? Why?

Ohhhhhh, You need me to sit still so I can hear You. Gotcha.

I thought I was being punished. I didn't understand. What did I do to deserve all of this? One day after being restless, angry, and fed-up with life, my Dad picked me up to take me to the grocery store. I was upset with him from a previous conversation, so he wasn't at the top of my list of people I wanted to see that day. But hey, there we were. The silence in the car was deafening. Then all of a sudden, he broke the silence nine minutes into the car ride and said, "You know the pain you are experiencing is not for you. It is for the next person to hear your story and your perseverance to be a testimony to them. You are not the first single mother, nor the last. Your situation isn't unique, but *your story* is. God will carry you, Danielle."

As I fought back tears in the passenger seat, I knew he was telling the truth, but why do parents always have to talk to you when you're still mad at them? Just let me bask in the ambiance of my anger, sir. As much as I wanted to hold onto that grudge, there was no way I could continue being angry after that. My dad knew how to get on my nerves and empower me all in the same sentence. He was a part of an amazing village that surrounded me.

An amazing village, THAT PART.

I was so focused on what was missing from my life—what I didn't have and what I wanted, rather than what I already had. I needed an amazing support system, and I had that. God trimmed the fat meat and strategically placed people in my life who served a purpose and poured life into my children and me. He removed those who were incapable of performing those tasks. I am forever grateful for my village. My children and my village show me what unconditional love

17

looks like. I evaluated the pros and cons of my situation, and surprisingly, my pros outweighed my cons, even during my adversity.

I was *placed* in the house with two toddlers, an unfinished dissertation, no car, and no clue when I would be employed again. All I had were my hands, and I placed them together every day and night and asked God to give me a peace that surpassed all understanding.

Man, one thing about peace is that when you experience it, you will do anything to keep it. Through my adversities, God showed me who He was, is, and always will be. I was a fool to place Him in a box and think my situation was bigger than Him! Baby, when He said He would make a way in the wilderness and rivers in the desert, He wasn't lying.

As I reflect on my journey, I realize I never struggled. He was there the entire time. No bill went unpaid, no meal was missed, my King has not experienced a seizure since he was diagnosed, both Kings are excelling socially and academically, I got a brand-new car engine for free, and I was offered so many jobs that I had to turn some down! My non-profit organization, Getting Over Adversity to Live Successfully and my LLC G.O.A.L.S. has emerged from my rubble and ash, Muva's snapback was nothing to play with, and I know for a fact that the networking and financial opportunities I have been given would have never come into my life if my story didn't play out the way it did.

In a world where social media and the unsolicited opinions of others control our lives, we subconsciously fall victim to edited versions of people and their lives and compare ourselves to a facade. Often while scrolling we get sucked into an algorithm of insecurity and comparison. Staying focused on *your* journey is hard. A word from the wise, aka Beyonce, "Stay in your struggle." I look back at moments I felt ashamed and laugh because I had no reason to be ashamed. I never gave up. I never threw in the towel. I never quit, and most importantly, I never took my crown off.

Check-mate.

I took that trash bag to the dumpster. I traded that bookbag in for an MCM and the work bag for a briefcase; the diaper bags are no longer needed. But I kept my bag of healing to remind me to be kind to myself because I am a work in progress. My journey has not been easy, and it is far from complete.

Once upon a time, there was a Bag Lady who didn't love herself. The lack of love she had presented her with obstacles she never even thought existed. Ironically, through her adversity, she developed a love for herself greater than any man could provide. Through her adversity, there were no limits to the story God had authored for her. She stayed ten toes down with her head held high, and the result...

Allow me to re-introduce myself. My name is Dr. Danielle Lynn King, b.k.a. Muva Xanny.

Memoirs of a Nomad

By Alana Griffin

Single

- only one; not one of several. unmarried or not involved in a stable sexual relationship.

What do you desire in your singlehood?

For me, it was to live my best life, and guess what? That is exactly what I did. I had the opportunity to travel as a flight attendant, seeing much of the country and the world. I was living my dream because I had always wanted to become a flight attendant. That is the joy of being single—being able to live life on your terms.

I traveled all across the United States. Being a flight attendant allowed me to live in the following cities: Ft. Lauderdale, Philadelphia, St. Louis, Indianapolis, and Columbus, OH. My favorite place to live was St. Louis, MO. The nightlife as a black professional woman was excellent. We would gather on weeknights and weekends and just have fun. One of my favorite events was called Jazz in the Park. Every Tuesday night my friends and I would gather our blankets, wine, cheese, and crackers and head to the park to hear live jazz music!

Just imagine a nice summer day, but not too hot. You are sitting on the lawn with your friends eating cheese and crackers, drinking your favorite wine, sharing stories, and enjoying fellowship with not a care in the world. The live jazz band is blaring in the background. My friend is feeling the music, so she gets up and starts dancing and singing the song. It's a whole vibe, so I get up and join her. I have not a worry in the world. I do whatever I choose, when I choose because I am single. No husband to get permission from, no children—only me. I traveled when I wanted and fell in love with it. It was not the norm for me to be such a free spirit and to live in so many places.

Have you ever heard the saying the black sheep? Well, my family called me the black sheep of the family, or a nomad as I recall. But guess what? I was living my best life, something many are afraid to do. Here are some memories of a nomad.

Scenes from a Single Mom

In St. Louis, as a single adult, my bank account was looking nice and fat. I went where I wanted when I wanted and spoiled myself at a whim. Imagine unlimited travel anywhere in the world. I traveled to the Bahamas, Mexico, all over the United States, Belize, Canada, Ghana, and Jamaica. You get the point. I enjoyed being a single woman, and I was happy and content.

Single life was fun, until it wasn't. It has its perks, and then it has its pitfalls. Lonely nights, cooking and eating for one. When your friends have a couples' night or a birthday party, you are scrambling to find a date. I dated for sure but was unsuccessful at love. Although the single life was great and I enjoyed it fully, I also desired to experience the next level: marriage, children, and sharing my life with someone.

Dating online was not as popular at that time. So, I told my family my desires so they could play matchmaker. I was preparing for my transition out of singlehood. To be the mom I needed to be, I decided that being away from my family and soon-to-be husband for three to four days a week as a flight attendant would not be ideal, so I decided to change careers. I moved back to Pittsburgh (my hometown) at this time. However, after some time I concluded that I didn't prefer cold weather due to my taste in warmer climates. So, being a spontaneous person, I searched for a warm climate, set up job interviews, and decided to relocate. Was it crazy? I had never been to Tampa before. Florida, yes, but never Tampa. Tampa was a layover, but that was all. Was I ready to relocate and live in another city? I decided it was time to find out.

It was Tuesday afternoon, so why was I not packed yet? I had two interviews on Thursday in Tampa, FL, and I was still in Pittsburgh. You see, I tend to procrastinate until it's go time. Well, it was go time. I didn't tell my family I was relocating, but I told them I had a job interview in Tampa, FL. That didn't go over well, but my mind was made up. I was making choices for the rest of my life, and if I wanted a family I got to decide where I lived to raise them.

Early Wednesday morning I packed my car with a few things, filled up my tank, and got on the road. It was an 18-hour drive, and I went without stopping for over 12 hours. At the 12-hour mark, I was exhausted, so I pulled over to a rest stop and slept for exactly two hours before getting back on the road. Remember I had an interview at 9 a.m. Thursday morning. The time was getting closer. I blasted my hip hop, gospel, and rap music to keep me awake. I keep thinking to myself, what am I doing? Yet, the decision had been made.

As I drove into Florida, the atmosphere started to shift. I saw the palm trees up close, not just on television. The air was moist and humid. I said to myself, "I am going to love it here." I pulled over to freshen up and change my clothes. It was 6:30 am, and my interview was at 9 am. I arrived on time, looking good for my interview, and I nailed it! I was offered the job on the spot. It paid well, but I wouldn't get paid for two weeks. That was a problem. I forgot to mention that I was tapped out of money. Flight attendant life never paid well; the tradeoff was the perks of getting to travel. I did have unemployment, but this relocation would take more than what I was bringing in. I had to start the job after clearances and a background check. Was I driving back home until then? Hell no. That drive took a lot out of me, and I needed to rest and recover. But guess what? I was in Florida, and I had already secured a job. I had a reliable car. I just needed to secure a place to live. I booked a hotel and decided to stay there until I had the green light on my job. I started to look onto Craig's List for a place to stay. I found an ad that sounded great:

Roommate needed, 5-bedroom house—you will have your own room and share a bathroom with a couple. $450. We also have a larger bedroom available for $650 with your own bathroom and jacuzzi tub. First and last month rent required.

I put in the request to rent the room. I got a phone call, we discussed my situation, and he agreed to allow me to take the room. His name was Frank, and he was a young man, a bit younger than me. He was very intelligent, and when I met him I found he had kindness in his eyes. I was honest with him about my circumstances. He said, "Well, here is the key. Move in immediately and stop spending money on hotel fees. Pay the rent when you can." A total stranger, he had just met me, and we vibed. I am huge on energy, and I thanked him for allowing me to stay. I was shocked, and with my housing secured I knew this was the right move for me. I felt at peace. I was close to the water, and the weather was perfect. You see, I am a Cancer woman, so I love the water. It gives me peace. I'm also a summer baby, so that's part of the reason I enjoy warmer climates.

"It's the best feeling in the world when the pieces start to fall in place." -Unknown

Now that my career and home life were established, I put myself out there to find love. Even though online dating was not as prevalent then, I invested money and started an eHarmony profile. I got many hits—men who wanted me to be their second wife, lawyers, accountants, and mechanics. I had a wonderful time being courted, getting to know these men, and dating, but I knew what I wanted and was not going to settle for less. I was also practicing celibacy, so the man I dated had to understand that as well. Being celibate narrowed down my list of prospective men.

Chile, I waited all this time and spent my twenties living my best life. I was in my late 20s, almost 30, and wanted to continue living my best life but with a suitable partner. I got pressure from my family as well. They all had children before I did, so they'd ask me when I would ever get married. They honestly thought I never wanted to have kids and that I would be a rich aunty forever. But they were mistaken. I did want to have kids—I just lived life on my terms.

After all of that, one man in particular stood out. He was tall, dark, handsome, intelligent, well-spoken, and lived in Tampa. He was a student at the University of Tampa. We hit it off, spent a lot of time talking, and finally met. He was such a gentleman. He was born and raised in Nigeria and had been in the US for several years. He courted me for several months before he professing his love for me. We desired the same things in life. He was a student, had multiple degrees, was a former doctor in Nigeria, and had no children (it was not that important as I dated men with kids, but if I found a man with all that I desired AND no kids—Chile that was a win). He was kind, well-read, exotic since he was not of the same culture as me, and he loved the Lord. The list of requirements I used to have was very long, so I could go on and on, but he met everything on my list. We continued to date as I traveled for business, and it was very important for me to keep my own identity. I moved out from my roommate's place, was doing well financially, and got my own apartment.

I fell for this man quickly and was swept off my feet. I love very hard, and that is part of the reason I was so guarded. I have so much love to give, and the flood gates open once I let the guards down. He helped me put my guards down and was everything I dreamed of. We dreamed together, talked about our families, wished upon a dream, and within ten months we were married, despite my family's hesitation.

"Your opinion is not my reality!" -Dr. Steve Maraboli

Married

- (Of two people) united in marriage

This was what I wanted. I wanted my own person, my life partner. We decided to move into a new apartment, since his place was the typical bachelor pad with the occasional roach and my place was small, with just enough room for me. Our new place was home, and it was large, new, complex, and beautiful. We had access to a gym and a community pool. Remember I was from Pittsburgh, so having access to a pool was a plus. I was enjoying Tampa. As I mentioned, my HUSBAND (I just loved saying that) was Nigerian. We already had conversations about him not having a green card but also not needing me to gain access to the country. So, three months into our marriage he told me his visa had expired and that he needed to go back to Nigeria for a few months. The struggle while he was away was difficult, and this was not what I had imagined.

After a few calls from him, he told me he was still working as a doctor back in Nigeria. Things just were not making sense to me, like why weren't things severed in Nigeria if you were in the US? You still have a job there? However, I listened to and trusted my husband. He sent money home while he was in Nigeria to cover our rent. I was unhappy that he had to be gone so long, but I loved him and wanted this marriage to work. He was gone for six months total. Remember when we were dating and he said he didn't need me to file for him to come back? Well, that was a total lie. I had to sponsor him into the United States and file for his visa. This was a surprise. They asked for my income documents and blood type (well not really), but they asked for everything necessary to determine if I could take care of him once he returned. This made me suspicious of his intentions, since this was not what he said to me when we discussed his citizenship.

So fast forward to his return: My feelings had kind of changed once he returned. So much trust was lost in me having to sponsor his return to America. Six months is a long time, and I was a newlywed wife. We were trying to rebuild our marriage. Rebuild back the love and trust back. The saying "absence makes the heart grow fonder" is a lie. I resented my husband. I felt duped. When he returned, I wanted the marriage dissolved or annulled. I felt he married me with ill intentions.

But three months after he returned, I ended up pregnant. I am a very loyal person, and I desired to have what I did not have—a two-parent home. I decided this would work and put forth an effort to make it work, even though I felt his intentions were not pure. But what could I do now, since he would be the father of my child?

The process of sponsoring someone into the United States is long. He could not work until he was granted a green card and work permit, so this was a hard time for us. I was pregnant and picked up a second job to cover the bills and other expenses we needed to secure all of his paperwork and prepare for the baby. He still insisted that a woman cook and do the domestic work. He could not cook; well, he could only boil noodles if necessary. I made his meals after I got home from work (when I say his meals, I mean traditional Nigerian food) and then made my dinner. Yes, I was pregnant, working two jobs, and cooking two meals daily. Oh, and he refused to eat leftovers. I always wondered why, but I think it's because where he was raised in Nigeria they only had electricity intermittently, maybe six hours a day, and had no refrigerator. So, leftovers were not an option as there was no way to keep the food fresh.

Did I say he changed once we got married and he returned from Nigeria? He was way more assertive. He was less affectionate and loving, which was one of our cultural differences. I expected a man to love me, or at least keep the same energy he had when we first married. When we were dating and first married, I felt he loved me. He showed me off to his family, and he said sweet things to me. But once he returned from Nigeria, he was different, and he would tell me I was his property. Many of the things I endured I never told anyone. I just cried and wrote in my journal.

This was my first year of marriage, and we were just surviving. I made just enough to cover the bills because he was trying to get into residency to become an MD in the States, which was very costly. America did not recognize his MD status in Africa, so he would have to go through residency again in the States before becoming a medical doctor here. We struggled financially, but he still sent money home to Nigeria to support his family. Side note: Families that live in other parts of the world think America is a gold mine. Some believe that once you arrive here you are awarded a pot of gold for landing at the end of the rainbow. But it is not like that. Here in America, you work for everything you get.

It took some time for us to overcome this. Our marriage took a huge hit. I was pregnant and working two jobs. It turned out my husband could not work for almost the first year of our marriage. We argued a lot as I felt he didn't prepare well. He lied, and that lie left us in a poor place financially and for me emotionally and physically as I was tired. Our son was baking in my oven, and I didn't need this stress. The doctor said our unborn was about eight pounds when I was only seven months pregnant, so I was scheduled for a cesarean birth. My husband agreed. I was so stressed because it was my first child. I felt my body was equipped to deliver this child, but I gave up my fight for a natural birth. We scheduled the birth of our son.

We argued daily—I was hurt, emotional, tired, frustrated, and pregnant. One night we had a huge argument, and I wanted him gone. Cops were called, and he eventually was told to leave the house. Ever since the OJ case in Florida, if cops are called someone has to leave, and if it gets physical someone is going to jail.

He was gone, but not long after he came back that night. He was so secretive, and I thought, "What are you hiding?" I felt he had another life he never spoke of. I could not prove it, so I never pressed. I no longer desired to be intimate with him, but that didn't matter. Remember when I told you he would tell me I was his property? Well, he would pin me down and have sex with me. I became so angry; I mean I almost hated him. His arrogance, his narcissism. He would blame me for everything I expressed. He told me that if I gave my husband sex and never said no, he wouldn't have to take it. So, it was my fault.

We would argue and fight, and he pushed me so hard one time that I ran into the table and broke my toe. I made up some story at work as to why I was pregnant and on crutches. Then my car broke down, I was well over six months pregnant. I was preparing for the arrival of our son, so I worked until I could not work anymore. I caught two buses to work. I was HUGE. The looks I got when riding the bus and walking a few blocks to work were mortifying. Yet I prayed I would get help from my husband. I didn't want to do this alone. I prayed he would keep his promise of learning how to drive to help. That never happened. I was a good wife, damnit, and I made two separate meals since my craving as a pregnant woman was different and he demanded his traditional Nigerian foods. But the stress was too much for me. There was a lot of mental and emotional abuse. At this point we separated; things got way too ugly.

We were now separated. At the time of our son's birth, he had found a job that did not require a green card, just a work permit, which finally arrived. The day before the birth he told me he had to work. "You have to work?" I asked. "So what? we are having a child!" He never showed, so my sister took a red-eye and flew in that night. I was so humiliated and heartbroken.

Our son was born on October 18th. He was nine pounds, 12 ounces. I'm so thankful I listened about having a c-section, as my son would have torn my body up. I cried for days—how could my husband not show up for our son's birth? He was so controlling, and he called when I just had our son. He threatened to sue me if I didn't give him his last name. I was so angry that I never finalized the birth certificate until the last day of my hospital stay. On day two my sister had to return to Pittsburgh. I was alone in the hospital. I had made arrangements to move out of my apartment, and I was headed to a shelter. I was close to being evicted, so I had to make that arrangement. Well, at least we would be safe. I was again humiliated.

I had to call a friend to come to pick me up and help us move into the shelter. I was a new mom, living in a shelter and separated! I was unable to continue paying all of the bills, especially after I took time off work. At the time of my birth, I had not been with my company long enough for them to pay for my maternity leave. I used all of my savings to keep us afloat. It was difficult to accept that my dream husband and desire to be a wife were not what I expected. Baby and I settled into the shelter. My husband would call, give me little money, and we would meet for him to see his son. He was now working. All of his paperwork was in, and he had an apartment and a roommate.

Me and the baby would go and see him. Yet, he never asked us to move back in with him and out of the shelter. I thought, "Are you okay with your family you said you loved living in a shelter?" But I honestly thought it would change him, make him hustle more, and make him miss his family. I was not prepared for this type of marriage. I felt unloved and unappreciated. I was so frustrated and disappointed. This was all a shock to me. My husband was looking for a better job since all of his papers were in, and since we were separated, he took a job in California. He up and moved. He abandoned us. Baby Gabe and I were left in the shelter to figure it out.

I stayed in the shelter for about six months. It took time to find a job, make the final decision, and move out. The place was more than a shelter; it was a woman's home. I had my apartment rent-free. I could stay there and get back on my feet for two years if necessary. The other mothers and I took parenting classes; we took infant massage classes. It was comfortable, and the other women I met there are people I'm still in contact with. But it was not home! Let's be clear. I was a married woman, with a child, in a shelter. He eventually asked us to move to California with him. I was not sure if I was going to relocate, and my family was definitely against it. But I decided I was going to relocate with my husband, who kept begging me to make this work.

Sometimes you need to listen to that still, small voice inside and listen to the counsel of family.

There's something about a man's ego and attitude when he cannot take care of his family. He was now certain he was in a great place financially to do that and afford me a few luxuries. He was highly educated, had multiple degrees, and was able to secure a great job. But California! At that time, I was working in the banking industry, and I was able to apply for a promotion with my job which relocated me to California. My family was not happy about this—for one I was already in Florida alone, and he was the only person I knew there. Well, let me take that back. I had built a community. A network of people I knew and liked. But I had no family in Florida other than my husband. The question to move was very difficult as I was still living in the shelter.

But like I said earlier I wanted a family, and as long as he was willing to put forth the effort I was also willing to try and make this work. We agreed that we would seek a counselor to get help with our marriage. He was my family, and our son was young, so I packed up and moved to Cali. Things were a bit different this time as he took care of everything, and as promised we attended marriage counseling. I tried to get past the hurt from being in a shelter, but he was a true narcissist and said it was my fault that we landed in a shelter. So why would I stay with him and then relocate? I honestly didn't want to fail. My singlehood was great, so I wanted to make my marriage great as well.

He did keep his promise. California was much better. He took care of all the bills, and I was able to use my money from being a business banker at my discretion. We had a nanny to help pick up our son from daycare. I had a housekeeper that came once a month to deep clean. We ate out every Sunday after church. It was a great change; except he was still a narcissist. Why did I expect that to change? He was even more emotionally, mentally, and financially abusive. I was all alone in California. He was so mean that he would get upset with me and not talk to me for days; however, he was so loving to our son. I desired love from him, which was something I don't think he could ever give me. I was not going to stay in a loveless marriage. He suggested I put my own happiness aside and stay married for our son, as if kids cannot discern when parents are not happy. It was time to hang up my fantasy of a happy marriage and separate.

"All human unhappiness comes from not facing reality squarely, exactly as it is."

-Buddha

Divorce

• The legal dissolution of a marriage by a court order or other component body.

We are in California; time has lapsed as we have now been married for almost three and a half years. And here I am, going through a divorce. I could not take it anymore—the control, the lack of empathy, the attitude that I was a woman and therefore had to do everything and was beneath him. Yes, he paid all of the bills, but I worked a full-time job too. I also had a career, but my career was not important to him. I bet he didn't even know what I did at work, or he didn't care. There was verbal abuse, sexual abuse, and mental and financial abuse. I would ask myself, "Am I going crazy?" He would say something like, "I curse you. If you leave me you will die." I would later repeat to him what he said, and he would act as if I was crazy, like I was hearing things. I started keeping a journal of everything that took place in the household.

I didn't make enough to live in California alone unless I moved to subsidized housing, but the waiting list was too long. I found an apartment and moved out. We remained separated for several months. I filed the paperwork for divorce, but he begged me not to file. I stopped the divorce proceedings. But he never fulfilled any of the promises he made. He did go to marriage counseling with me, and that was a disaster as he still blamed me for everything that could ever go wrong in our marriage. One day after counseling, the marriage counselor pulled me to the side and said, "You know I never say this or have said this to any couple, but I believe it is best for you to divorce." I knew in my heart that she was right. My husband just would not let go of the marriage. I always wondered why he was not willing to change. He never wanted to fix any of my concerns or try to make me enjoy being married to him. It was odd; he just wanted to co-exist.

After putting up a fight, nagging a bit, and complaining, he decided to take us on a vacation to Las Vegas, since it was our anniversary. This was his attempt to revamp our marriage. It was a spontaneous trip—we planned it out and had about two weeks' notice. I surprised him with tickets for Cirque Du Soleil. The first day in Vegas was great, and we were tourists. It was romantic, and we took pictures, enjoyed great food together, and drank a bit. The second night was the night of the event. After going out to eat, I gambled a bit at the casino, and since my husband does not gamble he just watched, looking annoyed asking how much money I wasted. We went back to our hotel to relax until the event. We argued, I told him about my concerns and hesitations about our marriage, and he flipped. He blamed me for being ungrateful and not appreciating him for bringing me to Las Vegas.

I was an "ingrate"—that was his favorite word to call me when we had disagreements. But this time he called me a "bitch." I told him if he ever called me that again I'd get my brothers to kick his ass, and I meant it. His verbal abuse was escalating. However, he apologized and blamed it on culture; he said he never knew that was a derogatory term. Again, nothing was ever his fault. He took a nap, a long nap. It was close to the time of our event. I started getting dressed. He didn't talk to me. That was normal. There would be days on days when we were married and lived together that he would refuse to speak to me. He didn't speak to me when I told him it was time for the event, and he continued playing dead or sleeping.

I was going to go alone. Remember I was a flight attendant, and I'm not afraid to dine, travel, go to the movies, or go to an event alone. Well, this time felt different. I purchased the tickets for my husband and I to enjoy together. They were over $80 a person. I was not about to waste that, but it was hard to go alone. I went to Cirque du Soleil and enjoyed it. I did get a few stares as I was the only person there alone. I ate at Emeril Lagasse Restaurant, had spaghetti—my favorite food—and then gambled. I kept looking at my phone expecting my husband to call and check on me. The show started at 8 p.m. It was 2 a.m. by the time the show ended and I ate and gambled. No phone call. I was heartbroken. This was supposed to be our trip to rekindle our marriage. He was trying to save our marriage, or so I thought. When I got back to our hotel room, he was asleep, and the same feeling came over me. This was not love. Did he ever love me? Why don't I leave him?

We got dressed the next morning, no words were spoken, and we left. I came back home, picked up our son, and went back to my apartment. We were still living apart. I knew that it was over, and I could no longer be his wife.

I was in California, alone and struggling. San Francisco is one of the most expensive places to live. My rent was over $2,000, and my soon-to-be ex-husband was now no longer the financially supportive man. He had things he had to do, he'd say. He couldn't help his son or even pick him up. That would have eliminated the extended childcare fee. He'd say that he didn't drive. I had to hire help. I had a nanny who would pick up our son and take him home. I was so tired of late fees assessed at the daycare. I was overwhelmed and financially strapped, and he was, in my opinion, living his best life. I was robbing Peter to pay Paul, but if I didn't solicit help, I would lose my job.

I filed the paperwork, and no trip or words could stop me. He hired a high-powered lawyer, but I could not afford one. He refused to help or give me alimony, not even a reasonable amount of child support. Thankfully the judge was not having any part of that. We went into the courtroom, and my husband barely spoke to me. It was so odd—he acted like we were strangers. He greeted me with a "hello" and sat several feet away from me as we waited in the courtroom. Our son was downstairs at the courthouse daycare. I had no help, and my nanny was not available during the day. He asked, "How is Junior?" My son is named after his father. I told him he was well, and that was it, complete silence.

My ex-husband was so spiteful to me, so vengeful. The relationship was unhealthy. The anger and frustration that I was divorcing him amplified. He was Nigerian, and many in his culture do not believe in divorce. A professional medical doctor experiencing a divorce is rare, and his image was now tainted. He tried to make arrangements with me. He offered to let me move back home if I didn't divorce, and he would support us as long as I waited and didn't divorce him. This was getting odd. Why would you agree to me leaving the state, yet never divorce you? At this point we had been married almost four years, and much of it was unfulfilled, with feelings of betrayal and a lack of love. "Is he incapable of love?" I would ask myself, but the answer was no. He was so loving to our son—gentle, caring, and kind. Yet turned out to be the complete opposite when it came to me.

When he learned I was going through with the divorce, he decided to take a promotion in San Diego. He was now eight hours away from us with no regard for his family or son, again. How was moving to San Diego the best decision for his relationship with his son? I was more motivated to file for divorce. We didn't have a home at the time, so it was an easy, simple divorce. He was making over three to four times my income, and with him being in San Diego I was awarded full primary custody with us sharing legal custody. It was final on June 16, 2016. It was five years and three months married to this man, and now it is all over! I had no regrets because God blessed me with a healthy, cute son. I was blessed in many ways.

"Sometimes you get to what you thought was the end, and you find it's a whole new beginning."

- Anne Tyler

Single Parent

- A single parent is a person who lives with a child or children and who does not have a spouse or live-in partner.

Where do I start? The definition of a single parent is objective. I would have described myself as a single parent, even when I was married in the same house as my husband. He refused to help with anything domestic, like cooking, cleaning, helping with the baby. So being a single mom was not new; however, it was more difficult as I was now responsible for all the financial needs. I had no support in California, so I decided to relocate back to my hometown in Pittsburgh, PA. I was embraced by my extended family and my siblings.

It was nice to be home—to be loved, to feel love, to be supported. But deep down inside, I felt like I had failed. My son would now be raised by a single mother, something I always wanted to avoid. I felt like I retreated. Did I? I always told myself that as a mother your kids come first, and this was a move about my son Gabriel. Had divorce and lack of support in California not been the case, I would have never moved back home to Pittsburgh. Don't get me wrong, this is my hometown, but it does come with cold weather, potholes, black ice, snow, hail, sleet, gloom and doom. So clearly, I only did this for my son.

Rent in Pittsburgh was a breath of fresh air. I rented a three-bedroom house, was still with the bank, and received a promotion in Pittsburgh. Gabe and I began to settle in. I will say it was not easy, and Gabe asked for his father several times. He wanted to know where he was, why we lived apart, and why didn't Daddy come with us to Pittsburgh. My desire to extend my family remained. I knew I did not want Gabe to be an only child. I knew I no longer wanted to be married to my ex, so I ensured that I didn't get pregnant. But now I was a single mother.

I don't know if any other single mom has dealt with this, but the unexpected divorce or breakup had crushed my desire to extend my family. I'm now a single mom, still working a nine to five, trying to stay healthy, date here and there and build a business on the side. I had not begun the journey of my healing, so I was not ready to jump back into a full-blown relationship. Yet, my biological clock was ticking. I never married to divorce, and now I have one child who keeps asking for a sibling or when me and his Daddy will have more kids. Kids do not fully understand divorce, and they often fantasize about their parents getting back together. And let me tell you, my son asked all the time. I decided to look for an alternative option to having a second child. I researched all options and settled on becoming a foster parent. You see, on my journey, I learned and am a firm believer that when you lack in one area, that is the area you give in. Example: If you lack love, you should go out and give love. If you lack money, go help the less fortunate.

I lacked a child, so I decided to support children. I became a foster parent, and the process was long. I took many hours of class training to become certified. Once I became certified, it took only a few months before I was placed with a boy, two years younger than Gabe. His name was Dimitri (Meech), and he was such a sweet and kind little boy. The moment he was placed with me, I instantly knew he would be with me forever. We connected. I looked into his tired, hopeful, and scared eyes, and I immediately knew he would be with me, my son.

As a foster mom, the biological parents are sometimes still involved, and Meech was close to his biological mother. He was born with drugs in his system, as his mother's major challenge was being clean. However, I didn't find all of this out until he was with me for over a year. It was a pill I had to swallow, and I had to learn to adapt and strengthen my skills to best suit my son.

We had weekly visits with bio mother, and she would show up when she chose to. She loved him, that was evident, but she was unable to clean herself up to gain custody of her son back. There were steady visits at my home—the weekly visits, weekly therapy, mobile therapy, speech therapy. We were adjusting. He was happy, and we were growing as a family.

Approximately 13,000 to 15,000 Pennsylvania children are currently in foster care and part of the child welfare system. Between 400,000 and 500,000 children in the US are in foster care each year.

Adoption

- The action or fact of legally taking another's child/the action or fact of legally taking another's child and bringing it up as one's own, or the fact of being adopted.

I never thought I would get here, being a mother to two children. Being a foster mom was fulfilling, but sometimes we go into situations and are not fully aware of the trial that comes with it. The path to expanding my family looked nothing like what I expected! You see, after three years they decided to terminate his mother's parental rights. That was hard for my son and myself. He knew his mother, so it was not something you can forget. What do I do now? Well, I keep a picture of his mother in my home, so she is forever with us. I also keep the lines of communication open, just in case she decides to reach out.

It was not easy, and as a parentless child Dimitri had his own set of issues. We are still dealing with unexpected trauma associated with the complications of his birth.

I have to affirm my kids and also myself.

Each day, the boys and I say our affirmations:

I am strong.

I am capable.

I am a KING.

I am a leader.

I am intelligent.

I am enough.

I am loved.

"Motherhood is a journey,

it is not clearly defined,

it's not the same for each mom,

it's not always easy

but YOU are called for this assignment.

I AM called to this assignment

Find and build your village.

allow yourself the grace to grow and develop.

I have found my village, my family.

I have grown to accept unforeseen circumstances and not allow them to disrupt my everyday life.

Our life is defined by moments... especially the ones

we never see coming."

-Unknown

Success

- the accomplishment of an aim or purpose.

The most important relationship you can have in life is with yourself. I have learned on my journey that life will happen and trials will come, but what is most important is how you respond to them. You can marry the seemingly perfect mate and do things the right way, yet life happens. I define my own success, and I set my own expectations.

I am an entrepreneur and have two handsome, healthy sons, a career I love, a great group of friends, associates, and a network. I am in a fulfilling relationship. I advocate for kids with special needs, I am a community leader and author, and guess what, I am just getting started. I look nothing like what I have been through. Without prayer, determination, my family, and God I would not be standing strong today. I am enjoying life and motherhood on my terms. These are the memoirs of a nomad.

You get to define what success looks like to you!

Alana Griffin

Scene II:
Frustration

There's No Room for Fear

By Ashley Whigham

Have you ever taken your eyes off of the road while driving? They say whatever direction your head is turned is the direction the vehicle begins to turn. I only know this because my ex-boyfriend wrecked my car on New Year's Day of 2014. Not because he was under the influence, not because he was inexperienced, not because he was speeding (he was actually only going about three miles per hour), but it was because he took his eyes off of the road. But that is a story for another day.

Anytime you lose focus and take your eyes off of the road, the chances of you being in places or situations you never thought you would ever experience increase significantly. I will not have a child out of wedlock while still having unprotected sex. I will not be a single parent while raising a child alone. I will not feed my child formula, and he will be exclusively breastfed. I could go on with the laundry list of things I always said I would or would never do that did not pan out, but that's not important. What is important is that I learned the reasons why I did the opposite are because I had never spent any time planning how I would intentionally achieve these goals or avoid certain situations.

You have to look at the reality of your current situation and your actions to differentiate what is actually happening versus what you hope for or wish to happen. It is also important to constantly evaluate if what you are doing is in alignment with your goals and values and if not, make the necessary changes to get on track. Another crucial point is learning and understanding the difference between a wish and a dream. The difference between the two is the work you put in to make it your reality. If you had asked me, I was supposed to be a doctor of some kind, happily married by 22, and a mother of three. I knew who I would marry, how my life would flow, and how happy I would be. I did not realize at the time that these were things I only wished for. There was no consistent work or effort put into achieving these goals.

More importantly, where was God in these plans? Some of these plans became idols, which meant I had made some room for God, but I certainly did not have him in His rightful place in my life. I began to use these wishes to escape from my own reality. Do you know how dangerous that is? I have literally spent years trying to create the idea of what I think my life should be rather than appreciating and accepting the reality and allowing God's plans to do the unthinkable in my life.

I remember sitting in a young adult small group at church when we were discussing idols and how to identify them in our own lives. Our young adult pastor at the time, Pastor Marvin Nelson, called on me (the quiet one in the back) and asked, "What is a nonnegotiable for you?" My response was "Marriage and children." Then he asked, "What if that doesn't happen?" I did not say it out loud, but in my mind I thought "God, I do not ask for much, and if there is power in prayer then why wouldn't you minimally bless me with these two things?" Honestly, I would be pissed if the marriage and children never happened, and I was a little agitated that he planted that thought in my head. I thank God that he challenged us that day because it was a seed planted. Now I can recognize when I am putting my goals, ideas, and plans before God.

Don't get me wrong—it has taken years, and I still forget because I have spent a lifetime with this unhealthy way of thinking. When you look at it biologically, there is a ton of research on the power of your thoughts and the chemical reactions we experience as a result of that thought, and the more a thought (good or bad) repeats itself, the more easily neurons fire. Over time, these create neuro pathways, which make it easier each time for those thoughts to repeat themselves. The reoccurring thoughts wear down the neuro pathways and make it harder to change. They become well-worn and heavily ingrained, becoming a building block for belief. Our thoughts become our beliefs, beliefs turn into action, and our actions turn into our results.

What happens when you do not take action? I can only speak from my own experiences—not taking action in my life has led to a lot of heartache, shame, disappointment, and feelings of hopelessness. I chose to write a few letters to share a small piece of my story with you but more importantly to put my pain and unfulfilled "wishes" into writing to memorialize them. I experienced a sermon by Bishop Donald Clay a while ago. He explained the importance of memorializing your trials and tribulations because they are not for you. He explained they are for those who come after you. They act as pillars to encourage them and allow those caught in their own storm to see that someone has not only been there before but also made it through. And that produces hope. So, here's my story...

Childhood Dreams

I am finally at peace with myself regarding the dreams that never came true. See, when I was younger, around five or six, I loved Disney movies. As my mom once put it, "They took the place of a sitter," not physically but certainly mentally and emotionally. I always dreamed of marriage and finding my prince, so I treated most of my life like a movie. I often acted on emotions, did what I wanted, and played whatever games, but at the end I still knew I would get my Prince Charming. Don't get me wrong, there is still hope for me, and I know my husband is out there. But, he will not be saving me from any burning building or awakening me from my slumber. I have learned that no one can save me but myself. I watched my childhood sweetheart get married and have children. I have also experienced my college love fade away into another relationship without explanation, and it was hard for me to see anything else but lost time.

What did I do to deserve this?

Where did I go wrong?

I thought I knew who my husband would be at the age of six.

Here's my letter to him:

Our families would talk about it, and little did they know, so did we. I began to live in a fantasy world where we would plan our future together. When his family moved away, we still kept in touch every few years. We would check in, and the feelings remained the same. I would get butterflies when Grammy would mention you were coming to town. I remember one time when I was around twelve years old and you were thirteen, I heard you were in town. I was so happy that my orange V-neck Aeropostale shirt was clean so that I could sheepishly show off the fact that I was no longer a little girl but a developing young woman. I hoped that you might notice. We drove to the meeting location of my grandparent's house, and I tried to look at and greet everyone equally in the room so as not to show how I melted as soon as I caught a glimpse of you. "He wears braids now," I thought to myself. I mean, honestly you could have gone bald and the feelings would have been the same.

There was no place to sit and catch up, but we always had our own language. A few words and your presence were just enough. Before departing, I remember you being eager to stand next to me when taking a group photo that you tripped over the coffee table. I used to look at that picture all of the time. I remember when our eyes would meet and we'd smirk. And then there was the memory of our first kiss, when you attempted to rewind my Bambi VHS tape and somehow the tape came out. You apologized of course, but then you leaned in and kissed me. I was so scared, shocked, and excited at the same time.

Years later, your dad came in town, and I thought it was odd for him to come by himself, so I nevertheless assumed you were there. He saw the disappointment in my face, shared your cell phone number with me, and told me to give you a call. Oh boy, "the call." I remember stepping outside of a party and my heart beating so hard I began to sweat while dialing your number on my mom's Chocolate Verizon cell phone (it was the weekend so the minutes were unlimited) and waiting for you to pick up. You answered, and I asked if you remembered me. You said, "Of course, how could I forget?" which created an instant high for me.

I remember when you came into town, and we went to the skating rink. According to my friends, you were the "ghost of a boyfriend" who had come to life, and they loved you. I remember us sitting at the tables looking into each other's eyes, and you taught me how to French kiss. And we practiced for hours, as most teenagers do. We never wanted to leave and separate, but somehow we would always run out of time. I recall you telling me that we would need to end our long-distance relationship because you would not be traveling as often, and I cried on my father's living room floor. I shared that your friend asked to date me, and you willingly gave permission, not knowing that I wanted you to say no and fight for us (because of course I think my life is a movie). To ensure I wasn't "alone," I spent four years in a relationship with your friend while we continued to talk about our plans anyway.

Oh, and then there was the time when you came back home for a funeral, except this time you had a girlfriend you were serious about. I knew just having a girlfriend would not change anything, but it was a little different this time. I remember talking, but it wasn't our language. I don't even think you noticed the black tank top with the lace I pulled out specifically to show off my back in hopes that you would think it was sexy. I realized that your girlfriend was heavy on your mind, and I re-adjusted to ensure that my most important role in your life was your best friend.

I remember the last real time we spent together going to Kennywood and being so nervous. I broke up with my boyfriend for a few days after learning you were coming to town. I know it's terrible, but I couldn't help myself. I remember you holding me as we leaned against the car. I couldn't kiss you because another man was also occupying my heart. You understood and held me. You said you would wait for me. You said you have always and will always love me. I told you I had many songs for you, but my number one was "Always Be My Baby" by Mariah Carey. You said your song for me was "My Angel" by Bobby Valentino. I never heard it, so you played it and held me while it played on repeat. This moment I will always hold in my heart.

Honestly, to become your wife was nothing short of a dream waiting to come to fruition, and this was the plan, our plan, for 18 years. I remember sitting in my off-campus apartment and talking on the phone for hours. This time it was different. You were serious. "So what are we doing?" you asked. "We can't keep talking about these plans and have nothing come of it." I went numb.

Wait, he is serious! I love him so much. Let's do it! That was the last conversation I remember us having. You know what happened next? I never had the courage to explain to you when we had that conversation shortly after calling it quits with him. I knew that it wouldn't work with him because you and I had a plan and a connection most wouldn't even get to think about, let alone experience. So here it goes: A few weeks after we decided to move forward in our relationship, I took a pregnancy test. To my surprise, it was positive. And no, my love, you were not the father. I called the father to let him know, and he was as excited as I had always dreamt of being excited. Wait, I'm a mom? I'm not married! This isn't your child though. How can this be? You've got to be kidding me. I have been waiting my whole life for this moment, and it literally slipped right through my fingers. I could not fathom telling you what I had done and how I had ruined our plans, so I just blocked you and shut you out, leaving your Facebook request on read.

When it came time to plan for the shower, Grammy asked to invite your mother, and I rejected the invite immediately with terror. For years, I would check your social media pages daily just to see how you were doing, as if it were the Post-Gazette I would read in the morning, especially when I felt down. I noticed over the years you found someone to love. I'd scroll and scroll and see that you were engaged. I remember sending you a text message, as of course your number was ingrained in my mind. "It's crazy how life works out. I just wanted to congratulate you on your engagement," I said. Your reply, "Well thank you, who is this?" I think to myself, "Ni**a it's a 412 number, you know it's me." "It's Ashley Whigham." "Oh thank you..." I honestly don't even remember what you said after that. Does it even matter? I'd scroll and scroll, and there you were on your wedding day. I was happy for you, but I still couldn't let you go.

I'd scroll and scroll, and I see you're expecting and then lost the baby. I do not want you to hurt, but I think maybe this is a sign. A few years go by and I do not check your page as often, but I heard through the grapevine that you are expecting again. Wait, does she have the same due date I did? Another sign? I thought I was fine and genuinely happy for you until one day I just happened to go on her page and see the Facebook Live baby shower. I lost it. Did not even see it coming and cried for hours. WHY AM I CRYING? Can I just let him go, please God? It hurts so bad! "I'm ok, it will be fine" is what I had to tell myself to reel it in. This is my closure. No way would I break up a family, not even in my mind.

Two years later, I hear you'll be in town with the family and stopping by my grandparents as usual. I tell my mom about our story and why it hurts, and she responds, "Wait, you are still stuck on that? You didn't even date? Never mind, how can I support you?" I was not about to try to explain something that she and honestly most people couldn't understand. I mean, we grew up in a time of transition where we could Skype, Oovoo, chat on MySpace or Tagged, and later Facebook. What was long distance most times didn't seem like it. Talking and texting every day. I know we only had a couple dates in person over the years, but for me they were enough to cherish and last a lifetime. So, I said, "Just be there." I anxiously pulled up to the house. I hadn't seen you in five years. I walked out onto the deck and saw your mom, your wife, your daughter, your brother, and of course you, my best friend. I asked your wife for a hug and neglected to hug you and not say too much, hoping not to come off as disrespectful as I know she knows who I am or that I was in your life. The energy made it obvious. I complemented your beautiful baby girl. I am in awe at the fact that you had a chance to spend time with and meet my son. I wonder what went through your mind. He's an amazing kid.

Of course, like clockwork Papa wants a photo before we leave. I was just as nervous as the last time when I was twelve but for a different reason. I wasn't sure where to put myself—not too close to you, but not too far away to make it obvious that I was trying to avoid you. But look at what happened, they forced us to stand next to each other with your wife in front of me. You want to talk about awkward. I could tell when standing next to you we still had that connection, as we were both trying to not touch or bump into the other during the picture to create necessary boundaries. I am so glad I chose to see you and your beautiful family that day, and I truly felt at peace. I thank God for that. Oh, and I did not get to say this when you were here, but by the way, it was nice to see you, friend.

Recycled Dreams

If you would have told me our phone calls would have nothing short of irritability, hostility, and I mean any "-illity" with an exception of humility, I wouldn't have even entertained the thought of you. Everyone else saw it, so why couldn't we see it? I remember when I first laid eyes on you Freshman year in the computer room while taking our placement tests. I saw your beautiful West Indian skin, tattoos, and fit and thought, "Wow, if that's what they're serving on campus, umm, yes please." Little did I know you saw me too. Now you won't even make eye contact when picking up our son from my house, and the sight of you irritates my soul. I feel bad when you leave because that's not how it used to be.

I remember when I fell off your skateboard just for your attention, or the first time we walked around campus all night just talking about life and you kissed me. I remember staying up all night with you, helping you complete a semester's worth of quizzes instead of completing my work and allowing my grades to slip to academic probation status. I remember the first time I smoked weed with you on 4/20/2012. I remember the first of many breakups with you, and you told me we wouldn't make it with you living in Brooklyn and me Pittsburgh. On my first visit I fell in love with your brothers and adopted them as my own. I always wanted older siblings. I painted a whole future for us and never paid attention to how uncomfortable you were with my big dreams.

I remember when you moved to Pittsburgh to be with me, and you had nowhere else to go. I remember you spending more time in my car than you would have liked until you got on your feet. I remember you being impatient and accidentally wrecking my car on New Year's Day of 2014 and me taking the blame when the police arrived because you were not licensed. Your apology was proposing to me at Walmart, which I quickly declined because you never did anything my way. Even just last year (seven years later), you surprised me and took me to Jared's, where we picked out engagement rings, never to return.

I remember our first pregnancy, and you helping me recall the grief I experienced with miscarrying when I unknowingly blocked it from my memory. I remember more breakups and finally calling it quits following one last "hoorah" after transferring to a new university. I moved on from my previous plans to be with him, and BOOM, three positive Dollar Tree pregnancy tests because when can a college student afford Clear Blue? I remember calling you as soon as I got the results and feeling your excitement all the way from New York. It was a time when I should be ecstatic while you were worried, but it was the complete opposite. You hopped on the next Mega bus and moved into my off-campus apartment, reassuring me that we would figure it out. Now it's only me figuring things out, now that you have your first girlfriend after our "decade of destruction," as I call it on my bad days.

Over this past year, I have watched you slowly drift out of not only my life but our son's life. It was painful for both of us for many and differing reasons. I have grown so much this past year without you, school, my job, or any other distractions that kept me from doing the real work. I choose to heal, and you choose to hurt, which is all I hear when you raise your voice at me or threaten custody as if you have a leg to stand on (boy bye). All of this tantruming to have overnights with your son, which would be perfectly fine if you would get him on weekdays, take him to OT, ST, or his extracurriculars, and more importantly if you hadn't just moved into your new place with your girlfriend of less than six months.

We decided that whenever we moved on we would keep our son at the forefront, never realizing I would no longer be a factor and you would leave me to lead a discussion with your romantic partner after fueling her with your side of the story so much that she aggressively dismisses anything I say. And you sit there quietly watching at her side. Does she not know who I am? How could you just sit there and not intervene? Was this a setup? I am learning the level of toxicity we shared and just how abusive we have been towards one another, not physically but emotionally and psychologically over the years. We both deserve better.

I remember when we would co-parent so effortlessly that strangers would question why we weren't together or married yet. Now the minute I answer the phone with a "hello," you turn your gaslight on. I'm choosing to heal, and I'm choosing to be better for myself and our son. I'm choosing to love you from a distance and accept that we were never meant to be. I'm choosing to thank you for our beautiful son, who has changed my life for the better. I'm thanking you for leaving and letting go of something that was already gone because I couldn't. Honestly and truthfully, you are not a bad guy. I care for you, love you, and wish you all the best.

Love, Bryce's Mom

Limitless Dreams

That was just a small yet important piece of my story. When I tell you I've spent roughly 22 years of my life worrying about whom I would marry and what people think, you might consider reaching for the nearest DSM-5 to make sense of things. Trust me, I've looked at possible anxiety, depression, and 100% REBT (look it up). Outside of those things, I had to have almost everything I was idolizing stripped away from me: my money, my romantic relationship, my education. I cannot even begin to describe the pain I felt through this process when I experienced it all at once. These were the three main parts of my identity, so who am I outside of being a student, girlfriend, and social worker? I had to begin the journey to figure that out, and believe me, at first I did not want to because I was scared of what I would and wouldn't find.

Earlier I mentioned that your thoughts turn into beliefs, beliefs turn into actions, and actions turn into results. Then I asked about what happens if you don't take action. So, I had to ask myself, "Why didn't I take action?" After some denial and digging, all I had left at the root was fear. So many decisions I made or didn't make were all out of fear. Fear of failure: I chose certain programs in college that did not have higher GPA requirements you had to maintain "just in case." I welcomed anyone and everyone who wanted to be in my circle for fear of being alone and wanting to be accepted by all. I stayed in one relationship while entertaining the thought of another "just in case." My self-esteem was remarkably low up until recently.

I have a long way to go, but once I started to see how valuable I am and have always been, I began to handle things differently. It's one thing for someone to tell you you're valuable, special, etc., but it's powerful when you begin to see your worth. In the past, my dreams were so rigid that there was no room for God's plan and no wiggle room for ordinary, unexpected life events. When things didn't work out as planned, I began to panic and tried figuring out how to fix it, when in reality God was saying it was time to move on or simply no.

Now, I still dream of marriage, family, and a fulfilling career, but I am giving myself permission to enjoy my journey of being single and loving myself. I used to hate hearing people say "I love being single" or "I am enjoying time with myself." It was crazy to me that someone could enjoy being alone, but I am starting to understand. I mean, if I don't want to spend time with myself why should anyone else? I am so many wonderful things and more, and I'm glad I am still on this earth to learn more about myself and allow my God to do the unthinkable in my life. These days my dreams do not have limits, and I know I will have everything I ever dreamed of and more in God's perfect timing.

A few Sundays ago, we had a guest pastor deliver the sermon. He explained how we should focus not on our past failures but on God's faithfulness. I know God has always been faithful throughout my life, so I'm confident in his promises. God knew exactly what I would be experiencing, and he also knew I needed community. I joined a single-moms bible study at my church. When I first received an email, I was embarrassed and thought, "Geez, how did they know I was a single mom? Do they just have all of us on a single-moms directory?" I later found out they saved the emails of the parents who previously attended the single-parent family camp. I also joined this writing cohort and learned how to share my story with others.

Believe it or not, I did not want to tell my story. I never thought anyone would read it. I also did not think I had "enough trauma" in my life and that others would think my life was easy. I now realize it's not about the many that might not get it or understand; it's about the one or two who can relate and are encouraged by my testimony to keep going themselves. I have an amazing community of women in both of these groups, and never knew I would experience a group of ladies in Pittsburgh who would pour into me just as much as I pour into them, maybe even more. True community.

It is so crazy that when you remove your idols and stop constraining your thoughts and dreams, you begin to allow God's blessings to flow throughout your life. In my opinion, there's one more important step to freeing yourself of your past. It's practicing forgiveness and grace, which are two things I am still learning. This step to freeing myself of my past and unfulfilled dreams was one of the hardest. You know why? It's because self-forgiveness is an ongoing process, and no one can do it for me. So, where did I start with this forgiveness? During this writing journey, we had to write a letter to ourselves, and this was mine:

Ashley,

Sweetie, I know your heart. I know you have the best intentions most days. You don't have to hold onto your pain, guilt, shame, failures, or shortcomings. Just let them go. I give you permission. The amazing life you have always dreamed of and worked towards is right in front of you. You know what's in the way? Your unforgiveness towards yourself. Right now I forgive you for being so fearful of making the wrong decisions that it leads to constant paralysis. I forgive you for the time you spent on small details of your life that kept you mentally and emotionally in the same place for years. I forgive you for setting higher expectations of others that you were unwilling to meet yourself. I forgive you for compromising your soul, values, and talents just to not feel alone.

Do you know how beautiful you are, both inside and out? Your heart shines so much that your presence, energy, and being are contagious. I am so happy you made it this far to see what I have always seen. You are empathetic, caring, intelligent, creative, loyal, passionate, God-fearing, dependable, loving, nurturing, resourceful, and intentional. Anyone who crosses paths with you has been blessed, which is shown in all your relationships with your family, friends, and community. The fact that everyone can say the same things about you in an intimate way is not lost on me. Even your enemies know your worth. Because of your constant integrity and kindness, you have seen change in them, and they have acknowledged your worth. Keep going. This is only the beginning. I love you, Kid.

Love,

Your future self

Whatever season of life you are in, it is important to learn how to love yourself. It means something different and looks different for everyone. Enjoy your journey and never think that where you are right now is where you will be in the next twelve months. Whatever your circumstances, you do not have to stay there—it's a choice to do so. If you're not satisfied mentally, emotionally, financially, spiritually, or physically, change it and surround yourself with like-minded people. That means you'll most likely have to try something new, something different. Don't keep doing the same thing because if it hasn't worked yet, don't waste more time on a "what if." Trust me.

In 2021, I was dismissed from my graduate program, terminated from my job of four years, and my son's father broke up with me after almost ten years together. In 2022, I have an amazing community of strong women who support me, my family, my friends, my own business (Always Live Well LLC), my own place, this book (I am a published author!), my amazing son, my faith, my sanity, love for myself, and my God. It is all about perspective. Think about the things that bring you the fruits of the spirit: love, joy, peace, kindness, generosity, faithfulness, gentleness, and self-control (Galatians 5:22-23). Our God is limitless, so think big, believe big, take action, and get your results. There's no room for fear.

More!

By Sonte' Grier

I was born to a single mother who only wanted the best for me. She knew firsthand what it was like to be a single parent, so the last thing she wanted for her first daughter was teenage pregnancy. My mother is special to me because she loves like Jesus does. My mother is educated and has a master's degree in social work. She modeled success as a single mother, even though she did it alone. My mother got pregnant with me at the age of 15. She wanted better and raised me to never settle. My father was not good to her mentally and was physically abusive to her. They did get married, but it didn't last. He vanished shortly after welcoming my only baby brother when I was four years old.

But, God chose an amazing mother like her to do it alone for my brother and me.

She put everything she had into raising us without one excuse. She kept my brother and me busy growing up—we were never bored as children. We were involved in weekly youth groups and stayed at church every Sunday. We participated in sports, dance classes, piano lessons, and summer camps. My mother even volunteered at the summer camps we went to. That's how hard she sacrificed for us.

My mother did her absolute best, and she loved us so much.

We felt the love and support from her but never her struggle. My mother is a warrior in my eyes, no matter the differences between her and me. She raised us on faith. She spoke life into us and taught us that we can do all things with Christ Jesus as our savior and center.

Still, I was empty without my father growing up. I wanted to know him so bad—I wanted to be a daddy's girl.

It never happened.

I could not understand how a man could bring children into the world if he wasn't going to be part of their lives. My mom deserved help, and she was robbed of that. She never even received child support! But she didn't bash his name or ever complain. She told me that I still needed to love and pray for him even though he was not present. She taught us to respect him.

No matter what, I still felt robbed of his love. I lost my identity due to not having his approval in my life, which mattered the most to me. I didn't understand why he stayed incarcerated.

I felt abandoned growing up. I faced rejection early in life by men. My father was the first man to break my heart. He missed everything. The bitterness and unforgiveness controlled my life, even though all I longed for was a relationship with the man that brought me into the world.

My mother was strict, but she was trying to shield me from the same mistakes she made. Despite that, I didn't get to enjoy being a teenager because I was so hard-headed. I caused my mother a lot of pain by making her a grandma at 33 years old!

I also caused myself a lifetime of pain.

I know what it is like to struggle because of poor decision-making and being addicted to approval and people-pleasing. I know what it's like to be depressed.

I was molested by numerous men starting at the age of twelve. Married men, men in the church I was raised in. I was looking for love as a result of the absence of my father, and the devil knew that. I couldn't hurt my mom or put her through that type of pain, so I stayed silent. It ate me alive in every area of my life. I wasn't brave enough to face the men who did these cruel things to me. I was so confused—one of these men was married but told me he would marry me when I turned 18! I knew it was wrong, but I could never get it out of my mouth. I didn't have enough strength to speak. I believed that God would eventually repay these men for their actions on His own. By keeping my mouth muzzled, I kept falling for counterfeit men.

The molestation caused me to be promiscuous and fast—I was in a hurry to be grown. I was lost, hurt, and confused growing up.

I had no business having a baby at 17.

I was a junior in high school with everything possible going for me. My mom told me to just finish school and believe in myself, but I still felt lost and incomplete. I met my high school love when we were 15 at our church's annual single-parent retreat. We both came from broken homes. We were young and thought we knew what love was. We were so naive and wrong. We were inseparable, and I thought we were going to get married. I believed him when he got me pregnant. I trusted and believed him when he said he wouldn't leave. I believed when he said that he would not be like his father. We ended up breaking up and going our separate ways for some years. I was hurt so bad that we fell apart in the middle of my pregnancy. I kept on moving through life after we fell apart. I felt abandoned and rejected, similar to the pain of never having my father, and I was afraid he wouldn't be there for his daughter.

Despite this, I was blessed with him being present as a father through his own life's ups and downs. We have a beautiful 19-year-old daughter, and she's doing so well in this life.

Moving forward to my 12th-grade year in high school, I got distracted again. I was working one night when a tall, dark-skinned, clean-cut, well-dressed, handsome fella walked in. He introduced himself as he complimented me on my beauty. I can't remember the punch line he used, but he asked me out to lunch. He smelled good and swept me off of my feet. He told me he sold cars at the nearby dealership. I was attracted instantly. He told me he was ten years older than me, but I wasn't moved by it. I was attracted to his stability, and we started dating and ended up together until after I finished high school. I moved in with him, and after two years of being together, I got pregnant with my second daughter.

This pregnancy was different; he was there for me. I thought I was so happy, Things were going well, and I was content with the family we were creating. But after some time passed, things started going downhill. Things were changing between us. The love was shifting, and there was distance. Two weeks before I had our daughter, he was going to leave me.

I begged this man not to leave me, and it was traumatic.

He packed his stuff as I wept. I remember grabbing onto his leg, screaming, "Please don't do this to us, don't leave your family!" He still said, "Sonte', goodbye, I don't love you, I love her." Then he said "I'm sorry" as he left and drove off. He left me for his ex he was with for five years before me. I remember being so hurt, feeling betrayed, and once again just confused as to why. I had our daughter in the hospital with only my mother by my side. She told me to pick my head up and to trust God. She always taught me that He has a plan.

I remember feeling like such a failure again.

On top of feeling depressed, I was in shock. He was there my entire pregnancy but still left just like that before our precious baby girl's arrival.

I can't describe the feeling of leaving the hospital without my child's father. It was a dark, empty, low feeling. I was humiliated as I watched the married couples or other boyfriends and girlfriends exit the hospital. Tears covered my face, but I knew it was no time to feel sorry for myself. I still believed that God had a plan. I pushed through the pain and the first year of my daughter's life without him.

We got used to the routine without him. I was working downtown and put her in daycare. I was depressed, but I still kept on going for my girls. I found a good groove in my life, but of course because I was doing better without him, he wanted to get back together. That was when I shouldn't have looked back. I should've kept going, but I wanted my daughter to know her father. I wanted my girls to have what I didn't have growing up. So, I gave it thought but not enough thought. I was young and naïve, and being ten years older than me, he took advantage of my fresh, young mind. I took him back, and I allowed him to move in with me in the new apartment God had blessed me with. We made careless decisions—a lot of them—based on survival mode. I fell for the idea of building a family with a man without a ring or commitment.

We had three more children over the next seven years, two girls and two boys.

He lost his job at the dealership, and he started going backward. I picked up job after job to keep us afloat. It wasn't enough for me, so I picked up a terrible habit that I had convinced myself was my new hustle—stealing from malls left and right. I became the provider, and it was draining and depressing. All we did was argue, and it was dysfunctional.

I was tired of having to be the dominant one.

I was tired of risking my life for my family alone.

We were not getting along. He was tired of being unable to provide, and I could see the depression in everything he did since his masculinity was stripped from him daily. We sat down and talked about numerous options he could do to bring in income. Since I worked during the day, he started Jitney driving overnight. Everything was going well, and we settled into a routine for a few weeks until he was out driving one evening and stopped calling or answering me. I fell asleep and was awakened at 3 a.m.

I AM HIGH ON CRACK COCAINE!!!

That was the text message I received, just like that. I rubbed my eyes and jumped up. Was it a dream? Was it a joke? I remember that night like no tomorrow. A gut-wrenching feeling came over me, and I suddenly realized it was true! Unfortunately, it was my reality. I dropped my phone, fell out of my bed, and hit the floor crying. Jesus, I screamed! My kids woke up asking questions. I couldn't speak, and I couldn't tell them. I wiped my tears and put everyone back to sleep, but I was still in absolute shock.

I was born in the '80s and grew up with a lot of friends who had parents addicted to crack cocaine. So, we knew not to touch crack since you can become addicted after one try. I couldn't wrap my head around his selfish decision to pick up a crack pipe. "Why would he? How could he?" I kept asking myself over and over again. The crack addict habit lifestyle is costly also. The last thing you want to do is pick up a crack addiction or habit when you're financially struggling, especially after you bring four beautiful children into the world. It made absolutely no sense to me! I was filled with hurt, anger, rage, and confusion.

I cried rivers.

The kids started asking more questions because they knew Dad didn't make it home. He was a very active father, so I couldn't hide it. I told the kids that Daddy was sick and in the hospital as he was placed into rehab after rehab. He could not get it together. I stuck by his side after he completed rehabs, but the cycle would just continue.

As I said before, I stole in malls to support us and keep our kids together. One day, though, he started stealing from us. I came home from work, and all of our TVs were gone! The kids' Wii game system that I bought—gone! I had so many nice things I got myself that he would steal and sell to

Plato's Closet. I was taking these things on the chin left and right. Stolen things were being stolen from me to support his habit. He would wake up out of his sleep and run to the drugs. He would disappear for days at a time and completely ignore me no matter what. His addiction had gotten that strong and bad. He chose to keep putting the kids and me through this mess. I kept saying over and over, "This is a nightmare! I wish this on nobody!" It was draining—crack cocaine is no joke. I watched him destroy himself as he deteriorated right before my eyes. But I couldn't just walk away, and I didn't want my kids to lose their father to drugs. I thought I could save him, but the longer I held on, the longer I put myself through it. The cycle would not end; he just kept repeating it over and over.

Finally, some relief came on my end. I was promoted to Kitchen Manager at Chipotle. I was working 50 hours a week and still going to the mall to supplement in between. I was still experiencing loss after loss. His drug use continued. He would steal my car left and right. I had to call out for days at a time. I knew I was close to losing my job behind him—it was only a matter of time. The last straw was approaching. He would steal my car and then leave it abandoned. I can't count how many times I had to report my car stolen, and the police found it for me every time. Then, he would steal all of my valuables! He even took off after picking me up from work one day. I left my purse in my car, and he took off without me. I was stuck at work, had no money, and couldn't get my kids from daycare. It was a mess! I felt worn out as a mother and was only in my twenties! I began to realize that I was drowning while trying to save my kids' father.

I began to lose myself more and more.

I tried to take care of our kids and him, but one night enough was enough. He got up to steal my car and go use drugs, and it was only by God's grace that I woke up and heard him in enough time. I flew outside, running down the steps barefoot in my nightgown. He was in my vehicle! I opened the car door and screamed, "Put my car in park!" He did not say a word. It was almost like he couldn't believe I caught him in the act. The look on his face was dead shock, as if he was wondering how I caught him so quickly. I knew it was only God that allowed me to catch him. The Lord knew I was tired; He knew I needed help and relief and allowed me to catch him!

I kicked him out of my entire life that day. I told him to do what he had to but not on my expenses anymore. I told him if he came back around my house or tried to break-in, I'd call the police and press charges to the fullest extent! That had not been something I had ever done. He ran down Black Street, a big long hill on the east side of Pittsburgh, Garfield area. I watched him disappear. I parked my car in front of my home. I locked my doors and my entire house entry, windows and all. I stayed up until the morning just to make sure he didn't return.

He did not return.

I prayed and thanked God that he got the point. God protected me every step of the way when I walked away and did what was necessary. I let go and let God have him. I trusted that God would heal him one day, as God only knows.

But the kids were beginning to act out in school due to their father's absence. It truly did affect them all differently.

My oldest son took it the worst. His behavior at school was out of control. He got suspended and sent home every week, fighting kids and running away from teachers. He was rebellious and defiant. I was often leaving work early in the middle of the lunch rush to pick him up. Even if we were understaffed I still had to leave, and I would have to call off due to my son's suspensions from time to time. My bosses were getting tired of it.

I felt hopeless.

You couldn't tell me that I wouldn't lose my job. I felt it to my core. It was only a matter of time. No matter how great an employee I was, it didn't matter because I had a business to run. With all this going on, I couldn't get the job done when these types of situations showed up. I had a lot on my plate these days with the children, and I started early every morning up at 5 a.m. to drop them off at daycare. I would get them to school and then open my store every day Monday through Friday. I felt guilty because I'd get off late and pick them up late due to putting in overtime at work and trying to get us back on our feet. It was a lot. I felt sad and like I was losing my kids and the connection we had. We couldn't spend much time together because my energy wasn't always up to par.

I was also tired mentally because I lived in my head. But I was determined to survive for the kids I brought into this world. I was severely depressed at this point. The anxiety and depression started to take their toll. I started moving out of desperation to fit in. I hung with people from work and even started to use drugs with other managers and staff. Wrong move! It was totally in the dark though; I kept it a secret from my family and friends. I spent so much time with the staff at my job, and it felt like we were a family. It was corrupt, and I was starting to see many wolves in sheep's clothing at the job. I knew it wouldn't end pretty, but at this point, I was in it for the long haul. I knew things were against me. My back was up against the wall, and I took every day as it came. I should have been taking the time to heal. Instead, I was self-destructing day by day. Everyone at my job was a young party animal.

It was beginning to be more pleasure than business.

We began hiring new employees, and one day in March 2013 we hired a handsome, tall, brown-skinned fella. He was shy but swept me off my feet with his kindness. His work ethic was off the chain, and he was like a breath of fresh air at the job. Everyone was attracted to his aura. He was a hard worker who went above and beyond, and we clicked instantly. One day, he saw me crying on my boss's shoulder and said he felt connected to me through my pain. I didn't quite understand what he meant, but he seemed heaven-sent. He told me that I didn't deserve to hurt and that he didn't want to see me in pain anymore. We got closer by the day. There was a rule that employees in the same working environment could not date, but we decided to break it. We began spending as much time as we could together.

We started dating.

I gave myself to him without making him work the right way, as I was moving out of pain from my past and desperation. He was on parole and coming home after six

77

years in federal prison, so he lived in a halfway house. We had late-night phone calls like we were teenagers. I opened up to him and felt like he was my best friend. I told him all of my deepest, darkest secrets. I never thought he was just storing info so he could later use it against me.

One day while working, I started feeling threatened by co-workers. Suddenly the energy was off, and I couldn't figure out what was happening. My heart raced as I thought, "Am I getting fired today because I'm dating my co-worker?" The truth was that in spite of what I did wrong or any mistakes I made, I still was the best at my job. I loved the job; I truly did. The customers loved me too, and I was up for a promotion to the next management level. However, all that came crumbling down when I was fired that day. I was falsely accused of not completing an important task that was the responsibility of another manager. It was her mistake, but they booted me out because of it. I couldn't believe what I was reading and experiencing as I signed on the dotted line of the termination paper.

I trusted God though, as I knew he would provide.

He did, and I was awarded unemployment. I still kept the romantic relationship with the guy from work. In fact, he told me not to worry because he'd share his paychecks with me. He kept his word—he stayed employed there while we were still in a relationship, and he truly did help me out.

One night we went out to celebrate his release from the halfway house. This was the ultimate shift in our relationship, and I was in for one of the biggest surprises of my life. We started at a few bars with some friends of his.

The night was young, and we drank a lot. We popped pills—molly, to be exact. His friend was flashing money he pulled out from his glove compartment, and my boyfriend didn't like that very much. I watched his face go from laughter to disgust in a matter of minutes. He was mad that his boy was showing off, and he thought I was impressed by that. The truth was, it was lame and stupid if you ask me. Anything could have happened, I thought.

His boy said he would buy us a room because he couldn't let us drive home. My boyfriend said, "Come on, we'll get home in the morning." We walked into the hotel. As we were checking in, two police officers were sitting at the desk. They lustfully stared me up and down as they chatted amongst themselves. We got the key to our room and headed there. After his friend went off to the other side of the hotel where his room was, my boyfriend pushed me. He started calling me a whore and a bitch. It caught me completely off guard! I remember that as soon as I put the key into the door I went flying across the room! He fought me like a man, and mind you he was 200 pounds and stood at six foot two!

The buzz I had from liquor turned off because I had to fight to survive.

He beat me like a prisoner in the yard, as if I had stolen or done something wrong. Someone called the police. They banged hard on the door. "One minute!" I yelled as I gasped for air. "I will be there, sir. Hold on!" He grabbed me by my face and said, "Pull it together, babe. I'm sorry, it was the drugs and liquor!" He said, "Tell them you got jumped at the bar before we got here, please babe!" I nodded as blood filled my mouth and poured from the top of my head. I said, "Ok, babe." I was so sad and confused as to what had just taken place that quickly!

I was scared to lie to the police and didn't have a moment to process everything.

I told the police I was using the bathroom, and they proceeded to wait. I wiped the blood. I fixed my hair. I noticed my earrings were missing, and my hair was all over the place. I did not look the same. I opened the door and took my chance with the police. They said, "Ma'am, we got multiple calls about a domestic disturbance over here." I lied to the officer and told him I had gotten in a bar fight upon arriving at the hotel. He looked as if he did not believe me, but he took my word for it and left!

Whew, talk about being scared out of my mind! "What the hell just happened?" I asked myself as I cried and broke down to the floor. I saved him from going back to jail, just like that? I thought if he went back to prison it was my fault, and I questioned myself over and over. He apologized to me over and over. Then he climbed on top of me, and I just let him have his way. I was broken and torn, filled with so much hurt and negative emotion. I didn't know it, but by not leaving him that day and allowing him to stay in my life, I signed a contract of emotional mental and physical abuse for the next five and a half years. As that day went on, I believed when he said it was the drugs and alcohol. He said he hadn't had any substances that long in his body after being released from a six-year federal prison sentence. I was blind to it, but I still knew enough to know a woman could never deserve to be beaten the way I was.

However, I made excuses to myself for choosing to settle for him.

I gave him another chance and moved him into my home with my children. I trusted this man and truly didn't even know him. That's the biggest place I went wrong—I thought I knew him. My feelings played tricks on my mind, and I made choices from my heart and not my head which saw the truth. He showed me who he was early on, and I stayed blind to it. I chose not to believe the negative. I overlooked his flaws because he accepted and overlooked my flaws. He was kind, safe, and gentle with my kids and gave them love and respect. The way he described his love for his own children, I never once thought he would harm any of them. I only knew what he said.

I gave him way too much of my trust too soon.

After some time passed, things started getting out of control. We would argue often. I would question when my intuition showed me things, and he would call me weak and insecure! He would control me mentally soon after; he had me so brainwashed.

One night he came home from work, and I asked him about another female at work. I had suspicions of them having sexual relations. He got out of the shower and beat me for 45 minutes straight. My 3-year-old son was in the next room and witnessed it all. He must have felt so helpless as he grabbed his earphones and tablet and jumped on the bed. He watched as I was beaten almost to death. I couldn't believe that he continued in front of my son. I thought he would quit! Every time I fought back, he fought me harder! I was so tired, but I knew I could not just lay down here and die in front of him.

I prayed in my head for the Lord to please get him off me and make it end. As my boyfriend beat me, he told me I would be the next girl on the news. All of a sudden, he took his medicine. He was on Seroquel, a powerful antipsychotic that made him fall asleep in a matter of minutes. I cleaned myself up, prayed over my son, and made a safety plan overnight. I woke up the next day and moved in with my mom—my safety plan. When she saw my face, I knew that she would immediately take me to the Zone Five Police to file charges. I was filled with many emotions, but I knew I couldn't stay silent anymore. I had to do something. "What if he did kill me the next time?" I thought. So many mixed emotions crowded my mind. I was so hurt and torn. I filed charges, and he ended up being convicted to 15 months in prison.

But I was not free. I got sucked back in through his phone calls from jail.

I swore it was over, but I was still trauma bonding with him. The abuse never stopped. I felt it might change every time he said it would, and he would give me just enough hope to hold on. The abuse continued over and over for years. He would degrade me in front of my kids. Soon it turned to me being dragged and beaten in front of the kids. I know that should have been enough! I'll never forget how many times he said that he hated me and that I would never be anything! I felt so low and hopeless. I stayed because I believed him.

He told me, "Nobody is going to want you. You're just pretty for nothing, and you have seven kids!"

I asked God why He blessed me with a son, the last son I had with him. I trusted that God could change him, but God can only change a heart willing to change. I was even verbally and sometimes physically abused while pregnant with his child. The stress caused me to give birth to his son five weeks early. I almost died in the emergency c-section. He was arrested for breaking the no-contact agreement he had in place for beating me in front of my son. I was sick!

Dèjà vu! I was leaving the hospital alone. Again.

I was disgusted at this point. I got into a depression and couldn't get out.

I raised our son alone for the first year as I waited for him to get out this time. He got out, and we picked right back up. The arguments began again, and the fighting and verbal abuse were back, as they never left. Before I knew it, the police were called left and right, and I was losing hope by the day.

Sometimes God will allow something terrible to happen to force us to let go! He will do whatever is necessary to gain our attention. He did exactly that for me. The signs were there, and somehow I convinced myself that this is what love was. The truth was, I never had an example of what love was. I thought it was to hold on and fight for what you have and whom you love. I was so broken that I settled. God showed me in October 2020 that it had to end and I had to leave. It's one thing to abuse me; however, when it comes to my kids, nope!

My daughter was violated by the man I trusted, the man I couldn't let go of. I cried so many tears because my daughter was brave enough to share it. My intuition had shown me that things were wrong, but I couldn't put my finger on it!

She did what I never had the strength to do. She is my hero. I forgave myself, and we are now receiving justice for what was done to her innocence. My baby is a chain breaker. I'm so thankful for her bravery and the courage to use her voice.

I have learned so much from each and every one of these experiences I have written about. Although I have no control over what happened to me as a child, young lady, or young adult, I can control what I do now.

I will always strive to ensure that my children are safe to thrive. God gave these beautiful gifts to me; it's not at all easy. I may be a single mother, but God has repeatedly shown himself to be faithful. I wish I could tell you that it gets easier, but to receive freedom sometimes the battles get harder. The more I turn from my wicked ways, the more the enemy fights my children and me. He knows the calling God has placed on my children's lives and mine. The Devil is threatened by that, as he should be. I let go and let God have his way, and he has been graceful to me. I put all my faith in him, and he's never let me down.

It will be 20 years this year since I have been a mother raising children. God has had his hands on my babies and me the entire time! His provision is like none other! My children were never without, even though they all don't have their fathers, nor do I receive child support. I have never been evicted. I've always had plenty, I've never lost my ability to care for people, and I've never been without!

Even through the ups and downs, I still have a heart chasing after God's own heart. God used each one of those experiences to mold my heart to love just as he does. I've been close to losing my mind, but He kept me! When I stepped away from the will of His life having children out of wedlock, He still kept me! He kept them all healthy, even through the many issues of life. He has never left us nor forsaken us. Even after I was fired and went to jail after boosting and stealing, the Lord was always there. Even when I made bad choices and my children followed, he still covers us! I can testify that he still showed his love for me through complete strangers. Income would come from complete strangers. It blew my mind that even though I lost a lot due to my criminal record, God allows me to be made new. He has shown me why He is God and God alone!

God still reached down at my lowest and dusted me off. He has truly given me beauty for my ashes. My faith continues to reach heights I have never tasted or seen. When I gave up stealing, it gave him room to move on my behalf. Blessing upon blessings so big I don't have room to receive! My life has changed for the better since I gave that up. It will be seven years on my birthday, which is when I was caught for the final time. I was pregnant with my last daughter and was in a jail cell. I knew I heard God say one word: "More." He said, "Trust me and walk away from this life of sin." I walked away from the lifestyle, and when I did the overflow of blessing and provision began. It has never stopped since!

I thank God for his "no" and what he did not allow. I thank God I was fired because it pushed me into the true calling he has for my life. I thank God for never leaving my side. I didn't understand why I ended up a single mother, but God is the father of all fathers and provides. He is truly the best father we could ever have.

God is showing me my value. He's remaking me after many years of insecurity and low self-esteem which made me prey to toxic relationships and abuse. I didn't value or love myself, and that's why I settled and stayed stuck. Today, I am a new woman who has put one foot in front of the other and trusted God to do the rest. I am not a victim—I am a survivor.

God gets all the Glory. Being molested and abused taught me this lesson: Hurt people hurt people. I forgive the ones that hurt me and those that persecuted me. Now I can live free in the promises of God. To the one reading this, you can too. You can overcome anything with God. You can do all things through Christ Jesus who strengthens you.

Philippians 4:13 "May God bless you and keep you."

Intermission

Dangerous Weapons

By Danielle L. King

Weapons of warfare.

Weapons of mass destruction.

B90 Nuclear Warheads. MK-17s... yeah, yeah... I know.

AK-47s. You got ya Rugers, ya SIGS, ya Taurus,' ya Smith and Wess...yes, yessss I KNOWWWW...

But what about the weapons of weakness?

Weapons that capture your soul and make you turn from yourself.

Weapons that allow you to muzzle your conscience with ease and renege on every, "What I'm not Gonna Do Is..."

Oh...you're going to do it.

Because that's what those weapons do.

Those weapons that help suppress every intuitive urge you have.

Those weapons that would have your mind doing something strange...not necessarily for a piece of change...but rather a peace exchange.

Inhale. Exhale.

Protected by a shield of faith, I am <u>A Queen</u> in <u>Kevlar</u>.

Rightful Place

By Teona Hall

I had a different face.

I had happy weight.

I was thriving, I felt alive. My joy filled any space.

I took the time it takes to place you in your rightful place.

As I ponder in my mind and try to trace what mistakes
allowed me to land

In this mental state.

I've been bombarded with distractions, I'm no match for these attacks that

Has me slipping and backtracking.

Pardon me, if I'm going too deep. But I'm losing sleep.

Staying up, praying much to you on how I can go back to who you have called

Me to be.

I have to quiet the noise. I have a voice.

Does anyone hear me speak?

I'm clearing the stage, making a way to place you back in your rightful place.

Surely, if I was fighting the enemy I can call on you and the heavens will quake.

But, when it's your hands that are on me.

Who can come and rescue me for heaven's sake?!

So in your discipline, I listen, I submit, I surrender.

I dismember all the idols that are competing to take

Your **Rightful Place.**

Inspired By Peppermint + Kindness

By Alana Griffin

This piece was inspired by a scent: Peppermint.

Minty, sweet, lemon. The scent reminds me of my childhood, age six. We grew up in the church. We attended multiple times a week. I remember my mom singing and praising in church. Since there was no children's church, us kids would have to sit there and behave during each service.

We would pretend to be the preacher, play thumb wrestling, and just be kids. When my mom noticed us getting fidgety, she would go into her purse and give us that red and white piece of candy. A peppermint. Mmm, how I loved getting a piece of candy. Minty, sweet, lemony peppermint.

Kindness Writing

She is a kind soul—brunette hair, rosy cheeks, and a good person inside and out. The love she has for people shines through. My prayer partner—so eloquent, wise, and peaceful. I know I can confide in her. We hold each other up. When I told her my troubles and woes about my child misbehaving in school, she paused, said, "Let's pray," and then asked for my mailing address. Why in the world did she want my mailing address? To my surprise, the next day a mug arrived that read "STRENGTH AND COURAGE." How beautiful—it brought tears to my eyes to know she is so sweet, kind, and compassionate. To feel loved. To know you are loved, protected, and lifted up.

Scene III: Freedom

Get Naked

By Nakeena Hayden

Can you imagine being with your mom every day, until one day you leave for school and then you're not anymore? To be honest, a part of me might think it was a good move.

It was better than being abused by your older sister! My siblings and I would get beat for no reason. But some reason was that we called a man we had known since we were little "Dad." We got beat for going to get ice cream with this man. She would make us play this game "hot beans for supper," just for her to find the belt and beat us. I would get beat for peeing in the bed. I would get beat because I wasn't a snitch and didn't tell on my other sister. I would get beat for visiting my mom when we had to live with her, when we were on punishment.

Not to mention, I'm the youngest out of eight!

It all started when I was only in the fourth grade. I got called to the office, and people were saying I couldn't go home or see my mom again. All I could do was sit there, cry, and wonder why this had happened. I was afraid. Did she not want us anymore? Did something bad happen to her? What was the cause of them saying this to me? I waited for her to come get me no matter what they said, but she never showed up. My heart just fell through my chest because what mother doesn't come for her children?

I didn't know she couldn't.

For a little while we moved in with my grandfather. I didn't even want to go to his house, but because he was family at first I was somewhat happy. He was strict and set in his ways, and the only person who had my back was my sister. He sent her to a foster home, though, because she was tough, never listened, and always talked back, but it was more like she stood up for herself and me. Before I knew it, I felt alone all over again. Sad, hurt, and angry. Why not just let me go with her?

I wasn't used to being by myself and didn't want to be either. I wasn't used to talking to a man about my problems or what my body was transitioning to, and I never had my dad in my life. I only had some man I called "Dad" because he was around when I was a baby. I barely knew how to talk to a woman about it. My body was becoming a woman, but there was no one there to teach me how to become a woman properly. I went to school with coats wrapped around my waist during that time of the month. I came home bloody with no money to afford what I needed, which he would never buy for me. I just was scared to tell anyone because I didn't know how.

I was always embarrassed about regular life things, but they didn't feel or seem regular to me because I had no clue what to do or how to do it. It was awful, that feeling of blood running down your legs in school, hoping no one finds out and makes fun of you. I felt an emptiness inside because I felt all alone and lost. When it was winter and around my time of the month, I had to be cold instead of warm because I had to wrap my coat around my waist to protect me from embarrassment. I would put toilet paper in my underwear to stop it a little, but that's all I could do.

I remember going into his basement and looking for paint for the only shoes I had—some Reebok Classics. I wanted to paint them for the first day of school so it would look like I had new shoes on. Oh, I hated it so much! I would sit there and paint with tears running down my face and wonder why I couldn't just be a normal kid and not have a life that was so complicated. Shit, I never made my own life complicated; it was being done by everyone else.

My grandpap had colon cancer, and when he had a relapse he couldn't take care of me any longer. So, I moved again and again.

At one point, I moved in with my aunt, who was my mother's sister, and her two children. I eventually felt like this could be home after a while. But I never got comfortable and would never take my coat or shoes off because I always thought someone would come get me. My thoughts reflected my reality, and I was always ready to get hurt because that was all I knew at the time. I really never had my brothers or sisters around, so my cousins became my brother and sister. But as time moved on, a situation happened.

My sister had come to stay with us! It made me so happy that I finally got to be with my sister again. However, my sister and cousin would always fight. They never saw eye to eye, and then one day they had a big fight. I thought everything would be fine—after all, who doesn't fight? However, when we had a Children, Youth, and Family Department check-in, she told them my aunt's boyfriend was living in the house. He had a background, so my aunt previously said he was her handyman. Because of that, they ordered me to leave her home.

And then I had to move again. I was devastated because I was comfortable and finally got to feel what a family felt like. It was happy, loving, and caring there. Being with my aunt was how I felt when I was with my mom, and I was close to the family because I knew and was always around them as a kid. I knew she cared about me. We did family activities, like for Christmas I would get presents and we would dance around the tree to Brian McKnight Christmas. Man, I will never forget! We would go shopping, and they called it a "girls day."

Just being around my aunt was beautiful. She was smart and determined, and she loved her children unconditionally. It was nice to see that, feel that, and have someone to look up to. We took family pictures, and it just seemed so real! She eventually told me about women's underwear, pads versus tampons, hair, nails, and hygiene. She didn't let me wear sexy underwear because she would say, "These are for women." I was still a young girl. My cousin liked to do hair, so she kept my hair up to date! I was able to like what I liked and hate what I hated. She never forced me to do anything I didn't want to do. She made sure she bought exactly what I ate, and she would make breakfast, which was my favorite. I could have those cheesy eggs all the time! Mmm, I can taste them now.

I didn't have to want for anything. Another memory was our game nights, playing Phase 10 and Pokeno while eating boiled eggs and hotdogs! I know that was quite a combination, but that was our "crack snack," as my cousin would call it. We would have cleaning days, and when we were done my cousin and I would have karaoke in her room, watch movies, and eat lunch together. My other cousin and I were like two peas and a pod, to the point where everyone would think we were brother and sister. We would get in trouble together, reward together, and play outside together. We used to have a curfew, so sometimes when we would want to go to parties we would ask to stay at our gram's house.

Although I had the time of my life there, I was still scared to ask for things and tell my aunt when I didn't understand something. I would just lie to myself and possibly make a fool out of myself, but she was there.

I was happy. She would take me to visit my mom so I could make sure she was ok. Spending time with my mom was all I ever wanted to do, so when I got that time with her we would have a picnic in a parking lot with some snacks. I would tell her about me, what I was doing in school, and the mentors I had. We would laugh and tell jokes. It wasn't much, but to me it was everything! Sometimes it also hurt because I knew I wouldn't leave with her. Our visit was for about an hour or two, and to walk away from the person you would die to be with was so heartbreaking. I was separated from my mom for a very long time from the ages of seven to twenty. I will get more into that a little later. However, I experienced all that good feeling and love just to be moved to a different foster home. I had to be liked, loved, and cared for all over again, but this time wasn't so pretty or comfortable.

I was then placed in a foster home on the Hill. This lady had one daughter, and the daughter had a best friend who lived with them as well. I have never seen anyone disrespect their mother the way this girl did. I was older than everyone, but I didn't act older. I still acted my age, which was 15 at the time, and I was in the eleventh grade. These girls never went to school and dressed like they were 25 years old. They would drink and smoke weed, and the mom would just let them. I absolutely hated this house! I knew this wasn't the place for me and felt it the moment I walked in. I just wanted to be liked and accepted, so I started following these two girls, dressing like them, talking like them, and going where they were going. My poor choices at this time could have ruined my life, but you could always tell that wasn't truly me.

One day those girls took me to a party, and we drank and smoked, which I had never done before. So, when I did it and started seeing three people instead of one, I didn't know what was happening. All I remember was trying to keep myself together so no one knew how high or drunk I was. That feeling was terrible. We then left the party to go to someone else's house, and they told me to wait in some car in the back seat. So, I did. Stupid me! They ended up leaving me there, and I eventually got myself together and walked back to her house. Not to mention it was like 3 a.m., and anything could have happened to me. I was so scared, but I was too high to be cautious. Two days after that, the daughter wanted to have all of us sleep in her room in the attic, so I did so. As morning approached, I felt someone touching my body, and I instantly awakened to find a boy on top of me! My pants were halfway down, my shirt was up, and my bra was unfastened.

I reached for my phone and cried out, "Please stop! Get off of me!" He kept going until I got in contact with one of my brothers. I cried out to him, and he said he was coming but never showed. The girls heard my cry out and asked what had happened. When I told them, they said they didn't know anything about what happened, but they really did and started laughing. The mom needed to buy her daughter some weed and tried to use my body to pay him off. I got my things and called a friend of a friend, and he came to pick me up. We went back to his place so that I could figure things out. I was so angry, hurt, and lost. I just couldn't think, and I had so many questions.

Why would this lady do this?

Why would my mom leave me?

How could my aunt just let these people take me without a fight?

Where the hell is my dad?

Why didn't my brother ever show up?

I felt unloved.

While I was lying there thinking about all this stuff, getting my things, and trying to find somewhere to stay, that friend of a friend saw me there watching *Drumline* in deep thought and forced himself on top of me. His weight was on top of my little body as he pulled down my pants, and I tried to fight him off of me but couldn't! I felt weak and lost and stared at the TV with tears running down my face as he held me down, whispered, "Gas ain't free," and raped me.

Feeling so weak, helpless, and tired, I never even said "stop." I just laid there and cried, and when he was done he said, "Here is a rag. Go wash yourself off because that's all your worth." I cleaned myself off with tears running down my face, asking myself why and left his house just wanting to kill myself. I felt disgusted and unloved, and no one came to help. No one even cared. What had I done to deserve a life like this?

When he dropped me off at my other cousin's house, they thought he was a new boyfriend and all smiled and giggled. Little did they know he had just violated my personal space, and they couldn't tell what I had just gone through. Even though he took something from me, I needed him. I couldn't have escaped the hurt I felt because I needed him! I couldn't even grieve what I had just gone through because I needed him. I thought, "Am I really this pathetic? Do I just let people do whatever they want to me and then act normal like nothing ever happened?"

The crazy part of it all was that CYF came to my school requesting I return to that lady's house! Instead, I never went back and went on the run. I can't believe they would take me away from my mom for using drugs but would make me stay somewhere I was violated at.

The system blows my mind!

Well, I didn't tell anyone. I continued smiling, laughing, and entertaining people like I always did. But deep down inside, I was ready to just end it all. I was waiting for someone to notice my pain. But it never happened, so I never looked back. I thought I could outgrow what happened, but I realized today that I never did. I am damaged because of that and not facing it when it actually happened. I wrote for years about this day over and over again, reliving the pain, fear, and confusion I had.

I became an alcoholic. All I ever wanted to do was party and drink! Being raped didn't stop me from having sex—it just made me not care with whom or why I had sex. I would just do it because I felt like people could just take it away from me anyways. My self-esteem got really low—I didn't know anything about myself anymore and didn't care to figure it out!

Growing up in foster care, you already feel you get cut short—especially if you don't even know why you're there. Listening to other people's rules, eating what they want you to eat, acting how they want you to act. "This is my house!"

"This is my food!" You already feel unwelcomed, overwhelmed, sad, and scared, and there isn't anything you can do about it. Hopeless! I know it too well.

I thought it was my job to get out of this situation. But how? I could act out! I could have sex to fill the void. But wait, when can you start having sex? If you start your period, is there anyone to show you? When you want to apply for school, how do you do that? Did I even have a birth certificate or social security card? Who was I?

I knew I wanted to be loved and cared for. I knew I would have loved to have a family. I could just settle for something because I had the power to make people better. Yes, that's what I thought!

So, that's what I did...

Being abandoned, misused, and unloved and having low self-esteem will make you put up with and do some crazy things, like underestimating your value to increase someone else's. Here's to the people who gave up on themselves while looking for love in the wrong places.

One day I got off the bus and heard my name called wondering, "Who in the world is calling my name?" Turning around turned out to be the biggest mistake I ever made for myself.

"Nakeena, the basketball player?" he yelled out.

"What's up? Do I know you?" I asked, looking at him.

"I don't know, but I know you!" he said.

"Oh, you do?" I responded, blushing.

"Yeah, I do, and I've been wanting you for a long time!"

"Oh, you have!" I said, sounding so dumb and naïve.

Someone noticed me! But I thought, "Whatever, bullshit!"

He had a nice smile and white teeth and was so chocolate! He had dreads. I could deal with that, but he wasn't my kind of dude. Still, he noticed me. That's all it took! Yes, I had plenty of male friends before, but this time I wasn't being extra or trying to be seen.

He SAW me.

That attention had me in my bag. The next day, my ass was walking down Main Street with some booty shorts and heels, thinking, "Who else will notice me?" I wanted all the attention—it was my turn! I had people whistling at me and cars stopping. Oh yes, I felt like the shit!

Feeling like the shit probably shouldn't have been my goal because he was giving less than what I deserved.

Well, what do you deserve?

At that time, I thought that it wasn't much! We started dating, and he was super whack—whack at everything. And I mean everything! Uplifting me, whack. Complimenting me, whack. Sex, well... He had just enough swag to pull me in, and he had money! It wasn't just about the money, though; it was the time he made for me.

Once he stopped having time for me, I got jealous. I got scared and didn't want to be alone, so I did something that none of the others had. I let him move in.

Move IN? You barely knew him! But I barely knew anyone who had me in their house. I got the house with MY income tax. Being about 19 years old, I got my own place after living with strangers for way too long. My mom was on drugs. My dad was never there. I was in and out of foster care, absorbing everything everyone else was doing.

But now? I thought I was rich! I got money, I got money, I got money hey hey hey... I'm smoking, drinking, having parties, just living, and loving that I had no rules to follow but my own.

After having a miscarriage, I ended up pregnant, again. I know, I know! This time I took a different approach. I was happy, I guess. I still didn't believe I was ready, but I was happy! A little person to love me forever! Something that I had been missing all my life.

And I thought my child could have something I didn't have—a mom and a dad!

Why not? This could actually work. He looked for me to remember. He wanted me to remember. This could be good. I have a house, and I have friends!

What else would you need? If this wasn't supposed to happen then, why did it? Twice! This was meant to be!

Did I mention that he was still in high school, and I'd already graduated? One day he went off to school, and I was home.

I went to sleep, and in the middle of my sleep I felt like I was screaming in my dream. I came to find out it wasn't a dream and was real! I was being robbed at gunpoint. I noticed the window was kicked in where the AC was hooked up. The dude kept saying, "Shut up, shut up." I was lying there breathing hard, and I was so scared and confused because I thought it was a dream when it was reality. I was quiet, and he told me to "stand up." So I did, and as I stood up I peed on myself! I was so scared with that gun in my face. I begged them not to hurt me.

I cried and prayed that they would leave. They made me walk around my house looking for money and drugs, which I didn't understand. Why would they be looking for drugs in my home? Well, when you let the Devil in, this is what you get! They asked for the combination of the safe, which I didn't have, but the safe was in my bedroom closet. They made me kneel on the floor, tied me up with a dog chain, and sexually assaulted my body with the gun. I had no answers for them as they carried the safe outside and told me to get into the closet. In the back of my mind, I thought that this was it. They will shoot this closet up and kill my unborn child and me. I waited there for about ten minutes in silence, hoping and praying they would leave and I would remain alive. I didn't hear anything, so I slowly opened the closet and ran down the street. I left my door wide open and ran down Broadway Street with pee-stained clothes to my sister's house. I banged on her door, yelling and screaming. As she opened it, I immediately told her what had happened, and her husband went back down to my house as I tried to get in contact with "him."

After that, I ignored him for a while.

I went back to the house to get some of my things and make a police report, but I really couldn't say anything. There I was again, putting everyone else's needs before mine.

How do I heal from this?

I didn't feel safe in my home, so now, I'm back at square one—homeless!

My friend asked her mom if I could stay with them for a while. She said yes, but I tried to keep my pregnancy a secret because just feeding me was enough. To know that I was pregnant too would be too much. I didn't have to tell her because she figured it out and made me feel as comfortable as she could at the time.

I lived there my whole pregnancy.

How could I take "him" back after he made me lose everything I'd worked hard to get?

I just wanted my son to have something I never did. I wanted it to work! But it was too much, from getting me robbed at gunpoint, making me lose my place, giving me disease after disease, and not giving me any rides to doctor's appointments. He didn't even show up to the baby shower the church gave me. It all started to feel so pointless.

Still, I was so eager to have this life.

And then life happened to me, and I named him Zion.

I house hopped again because my baby and I still didn't have a stable home. Some nights I would sleep in the park with my son, or I would go to other people's houses and sleep on their floors or couches. It just was all bad. I would always think that no one wants to hear a crying ass baby all the time, especially if it ain't yours. So, I never felt comfortable and always felt like I was a burden! Eventually, my grandma talked my mom into letting us stay with her. So, we packed our things and went to my mom's house.

I know what you're thinking. Why didn't I do that before?

It was harder than you think.

My mom chose either drugs or men over me, her child. If a man didn't want something, she would say, "Well, that man doesn't want no kids living here," as if she didn't have a say. I still honored my mom no matter what. To me, it wasn't her fault! But she finally stood up and said, "My baby needs me," and I did!

I needed my mom in so many ways!

At the time I was old enough to sign myself out of the system, so once I did that I went straight to her house. Not just for a place to stay but to fulfill my wonders and get what

I desperately needed. Even though I was older, a part of me wasn't. I still wanted to be that baby, that little girl she didn't get to raise. I didn't have to pretend to do that; it came naturally, even though I had my own child. Not only was she the woman I thought she was, but she was also the perfect grandmother. She loved all her grandkids, and to her it was like starting all over from not having her own to raise. I loved that for her!

Not only did we need her, but she needed me! When we first reunited, she wasn't quite her best self, and I hated that. All the medicine she was taking had her like a zombie, and I knew that wasn't good. I would take her to her doctor's appointment for support, and she loved that. I would do anything for my mom; when she needed me I would come running, no questions asked! She was being abused verbally and mentally by her husband, and once I moved in, I made it clear that he wouldn't be able to do these things to her any longer. Seeing her heal and know that I helped was great. That made the experience greater. She was like my baby, and I would always tell her that.

I eventually found out I was pregnant with baby number two. My baby was only three months, and now I'm pregnant again!

I couldn't believe myself.

I gave birth to my second baby boy Zakkai, all alone again.

How could I have done this to myself again? Getting pregnant the second time was a shock, but I couldn't go forth with an abortion. He promised to change and become a better person and father, so I stayed. I prayed, and I saw he could be different and better! I just wasn't ready to give up! But I was stupid. I was the one still providing, going to school, making moves to get our apartment, and borrowing money from people for ME to pay them back. Did I have any morals or values? We moved into our apartment, and eventually everything started to get better. Then, he proposed to me!

I said yes!

I knew he would change.

I knew things would be better.

The hope you have in people!

I was so blinded that my dumb ass paid for the whole wedding, and all this dude was handing out was diseases! My cousin just wanted me happy, and if this was the man I was going to marry then she would support me. She catered my wedding, taking care of the decorations and all. I was happy. I'm not sure if I was happy about whom I was marrying or just because I was finally getting married! I loved him, but I wasn't truly sure if he actually loved me. How was I supposed to know? I ain't never felt no love before. But we did it. We got married, and I walked down that aisle in my beautiful white dress with my boss and minister! None of my brothers were there. My dad didn't even show up.

"You" by Jesse Powell played in the background.

For him to want to grab me up like I was a snack before I even got all the way down the aisle, I was smiling so hard! I felt beautiful! We said our vows and took pictures with our loved ones, but then the unbelievable happened. How could I be so naive and blinded? First, I had to scrape money out of the card box to pay for the DJ, which was humiliating. This happened while he was in someone else's car getting high. Then I had to clean up the reception hall in my wedding dress just to get the deposit back. When it was time for us to dance, someone had to find him. The tears poured out as I sat on the toilet in the bathroom, pretending I had to pee and listening to that same song I chose from the heart. It played over and over again. I fucking hate that song! I couldn't believe this was happening.

This is supposed to be my wedding day! I'm supposed to be happy.

I instantly felt like I was drowning, but I put a smile on my face, got super high and drunk, and called it the best day of my life! I was cruising around the city with my girls in a limo, and I had just got married to my children's father! Already that was more than what I had growing up. So, I was winning! Well, that's what I thought at the time, and the people I was surrounded by let me think I was. But it turns out I went through all of that for no reason. He never turned the marriage certificate in, so the marriage was not real.

We split up because he accused me of cheating and doing all kinds of things I didn't do.

But once we split, you're damn right I did. I started doing everything he accused me of doing, even sleeping with the person he claimed I cheated with! It was on, and I was free! It felt so good not to hear someone tell me what to do or believe I had to stay because I didn't have anyone else.

And that was a lie because I had my mom now.

A part of my dumb ass missed him though, and looking at my two boys, I still wanted that family for them. I didn't want it with anyone else.

So, I took him back. Again.

All the hard work I put into that BOY!

All that I put myself through for that BOY!

The sacrifices I made!

But shortly after, he went back with his other baby mother and left me with two sons. I was also pregnant with his daughter, who he didn't claim. He did this while me and the kids were sleeping on another person's couch. We were homeless all over again! Life was shitty.

Now I was raising two boys, going to school, working full time, and pregnant. I carried twin strollers on and off the bus and walked with babies and car seats. I don't know how to cook, so who was going to feed these kids? I was stressed out! I went to school for criminal justice, and it took me six years for a two-year degree.

While I was pregnant and trying to get things together for the kids and this baby on the way, I ended up having a small stroke with my daughter. I went to the bank to get the deposit money for our little place I was getting, and I passed out at the counter. I woke up in a hospital with a neck brace around my neck and cords attached to my head for them to run tests! I had to get a lot of tests for the baby and me, and once I got released from the hospital, I named her Faith! She was born breached, and I had to get a c-section.

When she was born, I was afraid and unable to lean on the other half to be there for my daughter and me. I felt so empty, but I had to be happy. I had a daughter, my own mini-me, but I cried because how could I raise this little girl? I still don't know how to raise myself.

I told myself, "Just try not to fuck up!" as I looked into her eyes. Shit, I wasn't even sure if I wanted her!

My mom and some friends were by my side the whole way. At my six-week mark, I went back to work. I really couldn't do anything for myself, but I had to. I had to change diapers, clean, and wash clothes, all while healing by myself. People would visit, but I needed someone to be there! I couldn't walk for about three weeks due to an injury. I would try to find sitters, but the majority of the time they stayed with my mom.

This was the part where I felt like a failure. I got to walk across that stage for the degree I desperately wanted but never received. I still had 40 hours to complete in my internship and failed because I didn't have a sitter. The school closed down, so I couldn't find another internship. There went $50,000 down the drain for no reason! The hurt and disappointment I had within myself felt awful. All I wanted to do was be better than what I was handed. Why was that so hard? I didn't have a car, so I walked or caught the bus. Sometimes people from my church would let me borrow their car to go visit my kids because my mom lived super far. I was so grateful for them.

At this point, I looked at myself like a charity case!

We ended up getting a paternity test, and of course, the baby was his. He verbally abused me before leaving the courthouse, screaming that he wasn't the dad. It was pouring rain, and they watched us walk down to our bus stop to get on the bus. The humiliation that crossed my mind! It was just fucked up, and I wanted to scream so bad. I never imagined doing this by myself. I mean, maybe I had, but I never wanted to. I would always think I got cheated out of life—no mom really, no dad, no real childhood, abused, misused, abandoned, taken advantage of. But things had to change.

But what if it wasn't too late?

What if he was just trying to make me hurt?

What if I could show him I'm worth keeping?

What does she have that I don't?

My self-esteem was shot. Still young, but with three kids? No one's going to want you!

It was so low that I let my own family use me.

Forgive and forget! But I went through all that just to end up the other baby mom?

Keena, forgive and forget!

Still, I called around asking, "Why me?" No one had an answer, or it would be, "I knew he wasn't no good!"

So you just watched me throw my life away?

I honestly hated people in that season!

Life started to calm itself, I guess. I had my mom, I was talking to my dad, and I managed pretty well with the kids. I was getting comfortable and even got a new car. Finally!

Well, here comes the Devil once again. I finally started having a relationship with my dad for my kids because despite how he treated me, I wanted my kids to know their grandfather. He even came to visit me when I had Faith. To hear my dad tell me he loved me for the first time in 20 years and then two days later go into hospice and never hear from him again really hurt. I'm unsure if I just couldn't process my true feelings because he wasn't in my life or if my feelings weren't there. I eventually teamed up with my siblings and family. We decided to pull the plug on my father, and just like that, I was back to being fatherless.

Not only that, my car ended up getting repossessed. They wanted twice the money I owed and a fee for them taking it. More tears came because I knew I couldn't afford it. I was only one month behind! I could have had a ride, but I was prideful and selfish. I noticed when I went outside to go to work and my son said, "Mom, where is your car?" I told him it wasn't funny, but when I turned around it really wasn't there! I thought, "Oh my God! Why? What now?"

So, I strapped Faith up to the body carrier, put Zakkai on my back, held Zion's hand, and walked from my house to the daycare and then to work every day for a month! It was super painful—the kids would get tired of walking, and I would get so upset! "Let's go! Keep walking!" I would yell, cry, and stomp all at the same time! "Mom, my feet hurt!" "What you want me to do about it? Let's go!" It wasn't their fault, but every time I messed up, I blamed them in my head! It was always something because I couldn't afford this lifestyle. I didn't even stop to care or think about how they felt. The sacrifice, man! I couldn't believe it, and the funny part was we passed their dad's house on the way. No help, no reach out, no nothing!

I don't even know why I would think he would. He wouldn't even let my kids stay the night when my lights got turned off!

Nothing could stop me because I knew I had these kids now, and I've got to stay on my feet!

We ended up getting another car. I don't know how, but I did. My credit score was shot, and the car dealership man asked, "What have you been doing?" I was embarrassed and responded that I didn't know. No one told me anything about anything when I was younger! I was figuring life out as I made all these crazy mistakes! So, he made a deal. I only had $300 to my name when trying to get a car. He told me to come back with $800, and he could work something out. Buy here, pay here! I didn't know how to get this money, but I did. I surprised the kids with it when I picked them up from daycare.

I promised myself I would never put them back in that predicament!

My mind was shot because I was never able to grieve my dad. I had to work hard and fast and forget that I had just lost my dad!

My mom checked on me every day because of my experience with him, and she always made it easier to deal with things. Even with my kids or me being lonely she would always say that I was never lonely because I had her. She was my backbone, and I was hers!

I was happy here!

A year later on Christmas morning, I drove to my mother's house and found her unconscious and not breathing. As I stood over her crying out and trying to find her pulse, I couldn't gather my thoughts. One of my brothers was there with my mom's husband, but I had to be the biggest person and perform CPR on her as my brother and I pulled her off her bed. I immediately started pushing down on her chest and breathing into her mouth. I remember crying out, "Mom, please not now. I still need you!"

I performed CPR for about 25 mins. I can hear the operator saying, "You can do this. You're so strong!" and me saying, "I'm so tired." My brother kept saying how he didn't know what to do. I thought that I couldn't let her go like this.

I was so scared that I was shaking. I kept pumping and blowing, pumping and blowing. I was so tired and hurt because I knew my mom was gone and I couldn't save her. I felt hopeless in the moment, and then I felt guilty for years. It was left to me to save her! I sat there looking at her and admiring her beauty, trying to gather my thoughts and thinking that I really had no one now! Our relationship was so tight, and she was everything I knew she would be! I finally just got to hold her and watch her be still. To lose someone you want to be with so badly all your life and know she will never be back hurts so bad.

Just when I thought life was finally getting better for me, I was back where I started: sad, depressed, stressed, lost, and abandoned all over again!

I couldn't seem to shake this hurt, and it kept coming back full circle. It was deep and dark for about four years after my mom passed away. I still have unanswered questions about my past and unwanted feelings about things that happened, not only to me but to my mom. She was abused, abandoned, and misused, but she got through it. She was never perfect, but she was perfect to me. She was a single mom on drugs, lost all her children, and dealt with physical, mental, and spiritual abuse, but she was a strong, dedicated survivor and a wonderful mother and grandmother. Because of her example, I know I can't give up!

For me, taking care of myself is all I feel I can do. Or should I say, taking care of myself is what I needed to do. I know I can't be perfect and won't be perfect. I would love to love my children unconditionally and be more than just a working, tired, and stressful mother to them. Although I made it to motherhood, I didn't feel like a mother. This acceptance was hard for me. I wanted babies, but I was in no state to have them when I got them. I was so abused, hurt, troubled, and confused that the kids I brought into this world have been traumatized from the same thing I've been through—abuse. It's not fair to them to be treated this way, but this was all I knew. To yell when something is wrong, to force harsh words when being spoken to. You would think I would want the opposite for them, which I did, but I didn't know how to do that.

I want to be more understanding of a child's perspective because I wasn't able to be a child. How do you treat a child like a child if you can't remember being one yourself? I absolutely tried and am still trying to love unconditionally. I try to see them for them and show them that they are not a burden in my life. Being honest and being OK with what and how I feel are some of the biggest steps to the process.

Knowing who I am is completely different. What defines a person like me? Someone who has been through so much but never stood in her own reality to understand what she is going through or has been through. I know now that it's important to know who you are to become whom you strive to be. A mother, wife, friend, etc.—it wasn't easy getting here!

My advice is to face your own truth. It will hurt, but you can do it! You will continue to have blocks in your life without knowing who you are because you create character in all you do. If you don't know yourself, how can you strive?

Maybe you tend to follow everything you see and hear other people do and get trapped in it, but it's actually not you. When you get asked a question, do you have an answer that you've heard or seen? Or is your answer how you feel, how you see it, and how you endured it? In my situation, it took a lot out of me to answer questions because I had no clue how to answer them for me or understand them in a way I could elaborate. I didn't know who I was and what I liked—I didn't know it for me. I only knew how I saw or heard someone else respond or deal with it.

I know what my grandfather did as he cleaned and verbally abused and what my grandmother did as she nurtured and uplifted. I know what my mom did as she left but loved from afar, my dad as he never showed up, and my oldest sister who took the mother role for a short time in my life but physically abused me until I became empty inside.

I did all those things before because that's all I knew.

My mind was blank and my heart was ripped out of my chest when I realized in all this there was no unconditional love for my children. They were here, but that's it, they were just here. I hated this feeling I had about them. I hated realizing I could see their hurt from being treated like that.

It has taken five years to get myself together as I am currently am, but the woman being created is someone special. She is an upcoming real estate agent, an author, and a much more understanding, loving, caring mother. Not giving up could be the best thing that has happened.

I had the opportunity to get involved with When She Thrives three years in a row, and I kept blowing it off—until now. Writing this book helped me understand myself more and realize my strength. It gave me comfort in this person I am creating and gave me my worth back! My own words backed up my heart, and I began to feel again. I am a person, and I have feelings! I will become ten times the girl you just read about. I lived the pain, saw the pain, and dealt with the pain, and now I release the pain in healing! For that, I decided to write.

Get Naked

Naked, it's feeling free

But how free can you be?

He feels like he runs you,

He made you naked, you see!

With his unkind words, unfaithful doings, running back,
because you let him

His desires, with your desires!

To keep him satisfied.

You got naked!

Oh no, it's not just him!

It's people you let around you!

Abuse you! Misuse you!

Scenes from a Single Mom

Can you define what's true to you?

What happened? You were strong!

Don't let that man make you think it's wrong...

To love yourself

Be yourself

Free yourself

Care for yourself

You ARE A QUEEN!

Say it with confidence!

Speak life, the power of the tongue is dangerous

Please don't come to play with us!

See when a woman finds her confidence

There isn't anything you can do or say to her.

She no longer looks at the ground when she walks!

She picks her head up when she talks!

Those dark moments are erased! This confidence is here to stay!

Yes hunny get NAKED, get naked for you!

Those scars are healed and

We still have work to do!

So let's get NAKED!

Please forgive the unforgiving!

From an abandoned lost Girl to a Powerful Strong Woman!

Scenes from a Single Mom

Free Indeed!

By Teona Hall

My head was spinning, my body was numb, and my heart was pounding louder than the correction officer's black steel boots approaching the small holding cell. "Hall! Let's go!" she shouted as the door opened swiftly. My body felt like Jell-o from sitting on the rigid bench for twelve hours. I sprang up and rushed out the door. I followed the guard along with two other ladies who were being released. I couldn't use the phone to call anyone to pick me up, but that was fine with me. I would've walked home if I had to; all I could think of was my little boy and my precious baby girl. The last time I saw them was that morning when I dropped them off at daycare.

Suddenly, the alarm went off, a swarm of guards circled us, and my heart sank. I thought, "What the heck is going on? I am almost at the exit. There is no way I'm going back!" I sighed with relief when they charged after the lady in front of me. Supposedly, as we were walking down the hall to be discharged, there was a glass angel on a desk. The woman smuggled it and was caught on camera.

You've got to be kidding me! You are that close to freedom and blow it for a glass angel! I watched as they grabbed her and took her back down the long hall. I kept looking back as the guard yelled, "Hall! Let's go!" I was in disbelief, and then it hit me as I looked back one last time. Maybe she wasn't as nuts as I thought. Maybe she wanted to stay here. Maybe, just maybe, she wasn't ready to move forward and was afraid to do so. Whatever it was, it reminded me of myself. Staying when I knew it was time to go, enduring the pain from the mental abuse because of fear of the unknown. Being so close to freedom I could smell it, only to do something stupid to self-sabotage because I didn't feel like I was worth whatever it was on the other side.

I started walking faster. I didn't care what was on the other side of the door this time. I knew I wasn't staying here—this time I couldn't stay.

It took about a year to act on what I learned that day at the jail.

At first, I decided to take him back again.

I knew I would regret it.

But we are a family. Right? He loved us! He worked, and he helped around the house. The kids loved him. Look at me, convincing myself again and always falling in love with the potential. I never thought he would put me in jail. After all, I'm the one who caught him with her. I was walking home from dropping the kids off at daycare. When I saw the white Kia Soul in the Family Dollar parking lot, my chest got tight. I had a feeling something was going to happen. I walked past the store and saw him in line with her. I waited for them to come out, and I lost it! When the cops came, I was the mad black woman, and he was the helpless guy with scratches all over his face.

I can still hear his cold, stern voice. "Take her!"

Is this really the guy I fell in love with?

When I got out of jail, things did change. I was more stressed because of this woman, and he was less stressed because he no longer had to hide her.

I would have never thought the man I just had a beautiful little girl with and moved into a nice, beautiful home with would now settle for living around the corner in his mom's one-bedroom apartment so that he could be with her.

I felt so little, like that little girl who never understood how her mom could not stop getting high for her. I felt like that little girl who never thought she was pretty—I mean, come on, who has a face full of dirt scattered on their face? My grandma called them beauty marks...urgh! I felt like that little girl who had to wear her dad's girlfriend's off-brand tennis shoes for the first day of school. I felt like that bald-headed, skinny little girl that no one liked in elementary or middle school.

I felt rejected, unloved, and disposable.

I tortured myself by sizing myself up to this girl, who was 19. I'm 26, and he's 41. I felt old, disgusting, and washed up. I have two kids, and she has none. Her hair is long, and my hair is falling out. She has a nice, fit shape; my weight keeps declining. Then I would imagine him taking her to the same spots he took me and cooking his famous omelet for her. I know he told her he loved her, like he told me after the first week of making it official.

I couldn't take it, and I just wanted to die.

I thought my life was over as I stole my sister's car. No license, no sense! I drove around Mt. Oliver trying to spot the white Kia Soul. I went home weary, operating like a robot. My body was numb.

What is going on? What have I become?

My little boy and girl were the only things that kept me going. They were the only things that kept him coming back to visit, and I would use that to my advantage. After a while, he stopped coming around, and eventually I stopped expecting him. In that time, which was a few months, I gained about ten pounds and was expecting an income tax. He was prowling like a lion, but I was too busy living my best life that I didn't know he was waiting for the opportunity to pounce. Looking back, it amazes me how incredibly naive and broken I was. He started calling again, picking up the kids from daycare, and flirting. I loved the feeling of being in control again, the feeling of being sought after. It didn't take long for me to decide not to resign my lease and move in with him.

It was fun for a little while when I chose not to think. I didn't think about what happened to the other girl or about him putting me in jail. It was fun when I went on autopilot and numbed myself with weed, sex, and shopping. Now that I had him back, why did I still feel this void? Shortly after the kids and I settled in his place, he was at work, and I was home cleaning. I went through his bedroom drawers and found a sonogram with her name on it. The calmness I felt was scary. I sat down on the bed, holding this picture in my hand. I just sat there. I couldn't cry and had a blank stare. I knew it was over. The only thing that made me superior to her was that I had his child. Now the playing field was even, and I was prepared to accept the loss.

I looked at him differently. I looked at myself differently.

I finally started looking at my kids differently.

He was broken, I was broken, and my kids needed more. They needed structure and consistency; they needed a whole mother. I fooled myself by comparing my parenting to my mom's. I excused my weed addiction because it wasn't crack. I excused my absence in the home because I was physically there. I overcompensated with material things because of what I didn't have as a child. I tried to fill a void externally that had to start within. I was at a place so low that anything below was death, and for me that wasn't an option. My life up to this point became a blur, and it seemed at that moment

I actually saw things for what they were. I was at a place of desperation, a place of weariness.

I finally arrived at the perfect place, and the Lord had my full attention.

When I walked away, I left him on my mom's couch.

I tried to leave the memories, but they insisted on coming. The kids and I moved in with my grandfather. Even though it was time to move forward, my feet were slow to picking up the pace.

Honestly, I did not want to move forward or go back.

I just wanted everything to stop; I didn't want to move.

I was working at Pitt, the graveyard shift. I would get off work at 7 a.m. and rush home to get the kids ready for school and daycare. I walked my son to school and then would catch two buses to my daughter's daycare. I would get home and try to rest before picking up the kids and doing it all over again. I was so mentally and physically drained, and I would frequently wrestle with the thoughts debating whether it would be easier just to go back. Back to the relationship, back to the chaos. But was the little help worth it? If so, for how long and for what cost?

I decided to just push past the tears and keep it moving. My sister told me about a Thursday morning bible study at Allegheny Center Alliance Church. She said they had breakfast and then a study and that it was really nice. What did I have to lose? I thought, if all else fails I was guaranteed a breakfast!

I walked into the UP Chapel, which was adjacent to the main chapel the following Thursday and was greeted with smiling faces. There was a lady in particular I grew very fond of; she came up to me, introduced herself, and made me feel at home. She was gentle and kind. I needed someone in my life that was gentle and kind.

I came into that place broken beyond repair. My body could barely stand straight, and my mind was about as good as mush. I had two cups of coffee, donuts, a hard-boiled egg, bacon, fruit, and whatever else my 110-pound frame could wolf down.

Then I sat and listened to a speaker. All that food aroused my exhaustion, so I found myself knocked out with my mouth open, allowing the sweet speaker's voice to calm me into a slumber. I woke up just in time for the closing prayer and the breakup of the corporate worship into small groups. I perked up when it was time to go to the small group. The faces of the ladies, especially the kind woman who was our facilitator, energized me.

We talked about the Bible, which I didn't have much to talk about on this subject. The kind woman, Mrs. Claudia, asked how I was doing. I'm pretty sure she saw the despair in my face. I exploded with every emotion I felt. I could no longer hold it in, and it spilled over the whole group. I felt relieved, like I could stop running. I finally arrived at a place where I could stop hiding. The ladies gathered around and comforted me. I just needed to feel loved.

Scenes from a Single Mom

I felt the love from a community I had never felt before.

I started showing up every week.

Thursdays started to be the highlight of my week. I would eat, sleep, cry, and share. One lesson I learned pretty quickly was to just show up. When I showed up, even when I didn't understand, I always left feeling full. Full in my mind and body. After a month of coming, Mrs. Claudia gave me a small book, the Gospel of John. That book changed my life, and she changed my life. I remember staying up after I laid the kids down for bed. I started reading the small book, and it was really hard to put it down. I read the passage in about two nights and gave my life to Christ. I just remember giving him everything, and I asked him to please take all of the pain. I was hurting so bad, and he took it in exchange for a joy I could not contain. I wanted everyone to know about my new life in him.

Mrs. Claudia came to my job every Monday and had lunch with me. She would normally bring coffee for us both from home and a sandwich. We would chat and eat in her car, and if it was nice outside, we would go for a stroll. Our time always ended in prayer. I never had anyone who invested time in me and didn't want anything in return. Mrs. Claudia helped me see who Jesus really is. I had been to churches in the past and was probably baptized three times as a child, but I never experienced the love of Jesus. When I read my Bible, had my dates with her, and saw that the characteristics of a Christ follower I read and then seen through her were aligned, my faith grew. She was gentle, yet firm. Meek, yet confident in him. She helped me set boundaries that I truly needed in my life for the kids and me.

She modeled how my children were my priority after my relationship with the Lord. I saw how she put her family first and rarely compromised precious intimate time with her family. I finally had freedom in saying "no," in love and truth. I have always been a people pleaser; the more I had my focus on the Lord, I became more loyal to him and not men.

I was finally allowing myself to let go of others' expectations for me and embrace my new life in Christ. A life that was completely opposite of how I was used to living.

Mrs. Claudia was an answered prayer. I have always desired to be a better mom, but I just didn't know what that entailed. My standard of a better mom was better than how I was raised. The Lord showed me through her his standard of a Godly mom. She always talked with her husband before deciding and would get back to me to let me know what she could do. When she babysat the kids, she would follow up with me and thank me for entrusting her and her husband with the kids. She would let me know it was a pleasure to watch them. I just couldn't believe it! In the past it was nearly impossible for me to get a sitter, and then it blew me away that someone thanked me for watching them.

When the kids and I would go over her house for dinner, we all actually sat at the table, passed a bowl of food around, put our food on our plates with tongs, and asked each other to pass the bread and butter. We had delightful conversations, and she brought out a dessert. Seriously, I only watched this on the Brady Bunch or have seen this portrayed with happy white families on tv. This made my heart full. I wanted this whole experience, minus the white milk. You can keep the white milk—I need some Kool-Aid!

This was the first time that I was sober-minded as a mother. When it is written in God's word, the old is gone and the new is here. Meaning I have a new life in Christ, and I was actually walking out that truth. Whom the Son sets free is free indeed! I was enjoying this freedom in Christ; I was so enjoying myself. This was the first time in my life that I liked myself. I enjoyed laughing with my kids. I enjoyed cooking. I enjoyed going to the park. I enjoyed living, actually living without a drug or person to numb me.

I was gleaning so much off of the ladies at the Bible study who came along and supported me through my single parenting. I stayed in my word and believed what the Lord said about me. I believed in the Lord for a car and home for my family. The ladies would pray for and with me. I enrolled in different programs that helped with a purchase of a car, but they fell through. I continued to travel on the bus with the kids and just did what I had to do. The weather was getting colder, yet my faith grew stronger!

I remember the day; in my spirit I knew it was the day my prayer was being answered. I asked my stepfather for a ride to the dealership and drove off with my Goldie, my Honda Accord—my first baby! I couldn't wait to pick up the kids. Chay was the first stop. When he walked out of the school his mouth dropped, and I screamed that this was our new car in between tears. Then I picked up my little girl; she smiled as I put her in her new car seat. Shortly after this answered prayer, we moved to our new apartment.

I became a member at Allegheny Center Alliance Church, and then shortly after, my family and friends came to Turnball Lake when I was baptized. It was one of the happiest days of my life. I came from laying my body down as a living sacrifice to men and allowing myself to be taken advantage of, to now surrendering my whole life to the Lord and allowing him to take control. It was transformational. I started to volunteer as an assistant Sunday school teacher. The Lord gave me purpose. I showed up every Sunday delighted to serve the kiddos; eventually I was asked to lead the class myself.

Everything was going so well, but then something happened. What happened?

When I ponder back on what happened, I think of God's original design—how Adam and Eve had everything they needed from the Lord. They had no lack and were completely fulfilled. The Devil came and tempted Eve with what she didn't have. He told her she would be like God if she ate this fruit. The enemy tempts God's children in the same way; he uses the same tricks because they are proven to work. I knew I had everything I needed, but I wanted a husband to share it with. That was one of the biggest mistakes I made. I allowed that thought to fester long enough to give the enemy a foothold to deceive me. It wasn't a problem to desire to be married, but the enemy had me thinking like Eve that the Lord was holding out on me. I wanted that now, but meanwhile the Lord knew what I needed at that time and provided everything. I took my eyes off Him and started replacing the Lord's will with what I willed for my life. Pride comes before the fall.

It is written in 1 Peter 5: 6-8:

"Humble yourselves, therefore, under God's mighty hand, that he may lift you up in due time. Cast all your anxieties on him because he cares for you. Be alert and of sober mind. Your enemy the devil prowls around like a roaring lion looking for someone to devour."

This scripture gives me divine wisdom and understanding on why it's important to humble ourselves before God and acknowledge him in every way, not lean on my own understanding. The enemy came prowling like a lion and used that desire for a man in hopes to destroy me in every way. But my faith was what he ultimately was coming for.

I met him at work. He was a nice guy, or should I say charming. He was much older than me, but I seem to always gravitate toward older men while they gravitate toward me. The void of not having my father to protect and help instill value in me as a little girl made me susceptible to look for that in men who only came to neglect and devalue my worth as an adult. My father was physically there but couldn't provide what every little girl needs: acceptance, security, and significance. I'm grateful now that I've found that in my Heavenly Father, but before I found him, a girl was out here LOST!

This guy flirted, and I was doing well with just smiling and keeping it moving. I knew in my heart this wasn't God's best for me, yet I still entertained the idea of getting to know him more. I was intrigued with the fact that he attended church and had a stable job. The enemy is crafty; he knew what I wanted most, a Godly man. He knew exactly what to present me with, and I went straight for the bait instead of casting my cares on the Lord because he cares for me. I decided to lean on my own limited understanding because I thought I knew best.

It started with phone calls, and we mostly talked about the Lord. Then it was me slowly letting my guard down. I was addicted to marijuana and cigarettes my whole adult life. When I gave my life to Christ, I no longer needed those things to sustain me. The power of the Holy Spirit was more than enough. But the red flag I chose to ignore was that the more I gave this man my attention, I slowly started taking my eyes off the Lord. I desired to smoke again. I was still teaching in the children's ministry, but now it felt like more of a job than me working unto the Lord with pure joy. I wanted to hang out with this man. When I did, it was a different life than I was living, and I would do the very things the Lord delivered me from. The thing that was different was that I did those things with no shame before because the spirit of the Lord wasn't in me, and I had no convictions. Before I gave my life to Christ, I was okay with smoking and having sex. When the Lord called me to him and I became convicted, those very things became shameful in my eyes. I struggled with knowing what I was doing was wrong, but the power I allowed sin to have over me was so strong that I kept going back.

You wanna talk about how much of a wreck I was?

I don't know how many times I called it quits with him and meant it, but then I always found myself back at his house. Once, I remember I had a vision as plain as day when

I was working; it was a warning from the Lord. I would become pregnant by this man, and he would reject me.

The dream was scary, yet it wasn't enough to walk away.

A few months after that dream, my son and I grew pretty ill. I couldn't keep anything down, and my son had the same symptoms. The thought of being pregnant crossed my mind, but I comforted myself by knowing that my son was sick too and that we probably just had a stomach bug. We both went to the emergency room. The doctor gave me a pregnancy test, along with other tests they ran. I remember my son sitting on the bed while I was lying down. The doctor came in and said, "Well, I have some good news—you are pregnant." If looks could kill. I just laid there with my stomach doing flips, and I remembered my vision and cried.

My son was so happy. Meanwhile, I wanted everything to be over; I wanted my very life to be over.

Honestly, at the moment and in the months to follow, I was convinced my life was over. I couldn't live with myself. I dreaded telling him, for I had already foreseen his response. He was livid! I didn't want a baby as much as he did, yet it was completely my fault. The kids and I had just moved into a house, and we had no furniture—nothing. I would go upstairs to my empty room, lay on the blow-up bed, and cry. That little girl came back: the unloved, ugly, and rejected little girl. I would numb myself with weed in hopes of having a miscarriage.

I wanted my very life to be over. I wanted no one to find out.

What was I to say to the church as I'm teaching kids about the Lord and show up pregnant out of wedlock?

I would receive constant calls and texts about how stupid I was and that I was another single mother who would be on welfare. The enemy was coming for me big time. The shame and fear grew much bigger than my faith; that prowling lion had me right where he intended me to be. I decided to make that call to the abortion clinic.

I needed to quiet the voices of rejection, failure, insecurity, and despair.

I was convinced that was the only way out. I pulled up to the clinic and got dropped off at the front of the building. The protesters were outside rallying against the very thing I knew was wrong. I felt so humiliated. If they only knew that I was one of them. I knew what I was about to do was an abomination against the Lord, and I knew I was about to partake in murder. I knew this, but my wobbly legs kept walking with my head hanging low. My appointment was at 9 a.m., and the place was flooded with women like myself, some with their mates, family, and friends.

I traveled alone because I couldn't include anyone else in this mess.

I believe only one doctor was performing the procedures. I went through all the steps, like counseling before the procedure and being checked by the doctor. I was waiting to get the procedure done and move on with my life. I sat in a chair outside of a waiting room filled with other ladies. While outside of the room I could see the women in there and hear their conversations. There was a very loud woman in there talking about how many abortions she had, how the guy wanted her to keep the baby, and how there was no way. In my mind I was completely judging her. How could she brag about such a thing? What is wrong with this woman?

The Lord has his way of humbling his children.

I watched the woman walk out of the room and decided to go in as I grew impatient. It was after two, and I was still waiting for my turn. There was a notepad on the table so you could write to your unborn child. I remember picking up the pad, and the tears made my writing unrecognizable. As I wrote to my baby about why I couldn't keep him, the guilt and shame just bubbled and spilled over the pages. The woman came back into the room, and about three other ladies were in the room with us. They started chatting about what procedure they were getting. One of the ladies asked me, and I told them. The loud woman looked at me with her eyes as big as saucers and her mouth wide open.

"Girl, you do not want to get that one!" she exclaimed. "You are going to be in so much pain. That's the worst procedure to get."

The Lord used the big mouth of the woman I was judging to get me out of that clinic! The counselor called me back and told me I was up next, and it was now almost 4 p.m. I was in that clinic waiting to kill my baby for about seven hours. I told her that I wanted to switch my procedure. She asked if I ate anything, which I did, so she told me I wouldn't be able to switch. I decided to reschedule because there was no way I would proceed if I couldn't switch after hearing the horrifying details from the loud woman. I didn't call for a ride to pick me up, and my mom had my car. I just walked to the bus stop with the whole weight of the world on my shoulders.

I went home and drowned in my pity. I just wanted to die.

Of course, the phone calls started back up. "Did you get it?" I couldn't even answer. I had no strength to face anyone; I felt far from the Lord and God's people. The only thing I was close to was the voice in my head that couldn't escape. It's all over! My son and daughter were so happy about me having a baby, but I was so angry that I would get mad when they brought up anything that pertained to the baby. I didn't want them to be happy about the baby because I had no intentions of keeping it.

When I came home that day from the clinic, I was supposed to come home with no baby.

That night, I did something I hadn't done in a while. I forgot I had an option. I sat on my bathroom floor and cried. I just cried and cried. I cried out to the Lord, and indeed He heard my cries. I told him I messed up big time and wanted my life to be over. I asked him to forgive me and provide a way out. I said, "Lord, I'm in a big mess. This mess is so much bigger than me but not you. Lord, I need you. Father, I know you don't want me to get an abortion, but what am I going to do? The enemy is harassing me, and I can't stop the pain, Lord. I'm sick to my stomach, and I can't keep anything down. I keep getting these calls."

"Lord, please stop it! Please help me!"

I went to bed, and I woke up in peace the next morning. The situation sure didn't change, but I had my eyes on the Lord, which changed everything.

The Lord first gave me the courage to make it clear that I was not getting an abortion. The calls came to a halt, and I could think clearly. Then the Lord brought people around me to strengthen and encourage me through my pregnancy. The Holy Spirit spoke to me about stepping down from serving the kids. He had already placed it in my heart, so when the ministry leader asked to speak to me, it was no surprise. She was gentle with me and confirmed what the Lord had already let me know. She told me that after I had the baby, I could come back and serve, and she gave me a gift card for the baby. I could go on Facebook and share my testimony of my falling into sin and how the Lord had mercy on me. I also shared the news I was having a little boy and would name him Christian Jeremiah, which was inspired by Jeremiah 29:11: "I know the plans I have for you, declares the Lord, plans to prosper you and not to harm you, plans to give you hope and a future."

My baby shower was beautiful. I had so many people come out and shower Christian with more than he needed. When I went on maternity leave, the clients at work sent me off with monetary blessings. The Lord sure gave me the desires of my heart as I delighted in him. The enemy had intentions to steal, kill, and destroy my faith, but the Lord came to give me life in abundance.

When I think about how things could have been, I'm grateful for praying brothers and sisters who had enough faith for the both of us when I needed it the most. It was the faith of Mrs. Claudia, my Aunt Landa, my sister, my church, and friends who said, "Teona, I understand how it looks, but God is faithful."

They didn't shun me when I felt like I didn't belong. When all the odds were against me, they still believed in what God said in his word, and they walked it out. They showed genuine love and spoke his truth to me because they loved me. I am so grateful for the village of people the Lord has blessed me with.

Christian is now three; he lights up our whole house. I look at him sometimes and just cry. I hold him so tight and breathe in his whole little being.

In Romans 8:28 it is written: "And we know that in all things God works for the good of those who love him, who have been called according to his purpose." I truly believe in this scripture wholeheartedly, as it has been my reality firsthand.

Three years later, I am now co-facilitating a Single Mom's group at my church. I have worked at the University of Pittsburgh for thirteen years. I have walked out in faith and resigned this year. The Lord has been stirring in my spirit for a while to stay home and focus on the kids. He has gifted me with the passion for writing and also has given me a vision to start a ministry called Pink Talk, which stands on Psalm 66:16: "Come and hear all you who fear God and let me tell you what he has done for me." Pink Talk is a ministry to help believers like myself who struggle with generational cycles that have caused them to be stagnant and deficient in their walk with the Lord. There is power in our testimony, and through my own struggle and experiences as a believer I am qualified to help others embrace their complete freedom in Christ and have the courage to walk it out in faith.

I just want to be sold out for Jesus!

I want people to know that this little broken-down girl who was so far beyond repair is redeemed, restored, and made new by the Lord's saving grace. If He has done it for me, He shows no partiality. He indeed is willing and waiting to do it for you. For who the Son sets free is free indeed!

Scriptural Freedom Guide

Whom the Son sets free is free indeed. John 8:36

Free to Forgive. Colossians 3:13-14

Free to Love. Galatians 5:13-14

Free to walk in Power, Love, and a Sound Mind. 2 Timothy 1:7

Free to have Peace. John 6:33 John 14:27

Free to bear Fruit—Fruit that will last. John 14:27

Free access the Fruit of the Spirit: Love, joy, peace patience, kindness, goodness, faithfulness, gentleness,

and self-control. Galatians 5:22

Free to be a friend of Jesus. John 15:15

Free to remain in him. John 15:5

Free to do Greater works than Christ when he was here on Earth, and even greater things than these because he went to the Father, those who believe. John 14:12

Scenes from a Single Mom

Featured Author

Teona Hall

Teona Hall is a mother of three who aspires to look more and more like Jesus daily. Her greatest accomplishment to date has been being obedient and trusting God's call to leave her nine-to-five job to do Kingdom Work: raising her children and being used as a vessel to bring forth "Pink Talk," a ministry to help believers embrace complete freedom in Christ and the courage to walk it out in faith! She is currently in school to obtain a degree in Social Work.

Her favorite scripture is 1 Corinthians 10:13 "No temptation has overtaken you except what is known to man. And God is Faithful; he will not allow you to be tempted beyond what you can bear. But when you are tempted he will provide a way out so you can stand up under it." This scripture has helped her overcome addiction as she recited it out loud countless times, fighting back against thoughts of unworthiness.

About the Authors

Sonte' Grier

 Sonte' Grier is a God-fearing, proud mother of seven. She is committed to walking not by sight, but by faith. She knows there isn't anything she can't overcome as long as she maintains her faith in God.

She was born and raised in Pittsburgh, PA. She loves to read and collect journals to write in. She hopes to soon create her own Christian lifestyle brand featuring Prayer and Testimony Journals and a Faith-based Christian t-shirt and hat line. She also has a passion for cooking and a love to serve others.

Sonte' believes she is called to women's ministry and is striving to do whatever God calls her to do. She loves hard and loves to give in whatever way possible. She is a firm believer in Philippians 4:13 "You can do all things through Christ who strengthens you."

Most importantly, she is a woman chasing after God's own heart. She desires to leave a legacy of serving others, helping anyone she can through the things she has walked through herself.

Alana Griffin

Alana Griffin is a proud mother of two boys. She has a passion for her community which has allowed her to be seated on several community boards. Part of her community work is championing equality for mothers and advocating for special needs children, workforce development, and youth empowerment.

Alana is an entrepreneur and has a positive affirmation apparel line. She is an author, an avid reader, and also a stock trader. In her free time, Alana enjoys traveling, cooking new recipes, reading, and spending time with her family and friends.

Nakeena Hayden

Nakeena is a strong-willed woman and proud mother of three: two sons and a daughter. She was born and raised in Pittsburgh, PA and graduated from Langley High School. Being a victim of all abuse, she stands firm in caring for herself daily and never giving up. With the strength it took to overcome her hardships, she feels everything else is a piece of pie.

Her mission in life is to move past her hardships to become the best version of herself. Her vision is to live a life where she is a reflection of overcoming hardship to young women.

She is pursuing a career in real estate and has her own investment company called NHER Properties. In her spare time, she travels with her daughter to cheer and dance competitions and runs to baseball, football, and basketball games with the boys. There is nothing she won't do for her kids—for her, they are the best part!

Nakeena's promise to herself is to stop acting like she's afraid of her own power and move as her highest self, completely and unapologetically.

Nakeena's advice to you: Where it feels like the end, it's only the beginning. Get out of your own way!

Danielle King

Danielle has taken on many roles, but her most important role to date has been being a mother to three-year-old twins, Gavin and Carter King.

Danielle began her single mother journey in 2019 during her second year as a doctoral student at Duquesne University, and that's when perseverance became her.

Through the whoas and lows of life, love, and legacy, she continuously pushed through her adversities to become an amazing mother, published author, doctoral graduate, founder and CEO of G.O.A.L.S. LLC and Getting Over Adversity to Live Successfully, Inc., and homeowner.

Through this time, she has obtained and maintained the courage, confidence, and class to be beautifully crazy and unapologetically her.

Danielle is an avid peace seeker because she believes "peace is the real bag." She enjoys the sun on her face, smiling until her cheeks hurt, laughing until her sides ache, and experiencing every aspect of life with those she loves the most.

When in doubt, put on that **JRIP**:

Jeremiah 29:11 (YOUR Prosperous Plans)

Romans 12:2 (Don't get caught up in the world's Janky Promoters)

Isaiah 55:8-9 (God is bigger than your thoughts, get out ya head)

Philippians 4:6-7 (Don't be anxious, Boo)

Ashley Whigham

Ashley Whigham, 29, is a mother, daughter, sister, niece, and friend. She is a Pittsburgh native. She has an Associate of Science in Early Education and Child Development from Community College of Allegheny County and a Bachelor of Science in Child Development and Family Relations from Indiana University of Pennsylvania.

Over the past decade, Ashley has worked professionally with children and families of various backgrounds and abilities. She continues her work within the community by volunteering with local organizations, as well as through her own small business Always Live Well LLC. Ashley has taken her own hardships in the past to create a business to address people's issues from a holistic and needs-based approach.

Ashley is a woman of faith who strives to keep God at the center of her work. This is Ashley's first publication, and she is proud to use her academic, personal, and professional experiences to share her story in the hopes of encouraging her readers.

CPSIA information can be obtained
at www.ICGtesting.com
Printed in the USA
BVHW042158150822
644695BV00003B/51